SNOW FOOD

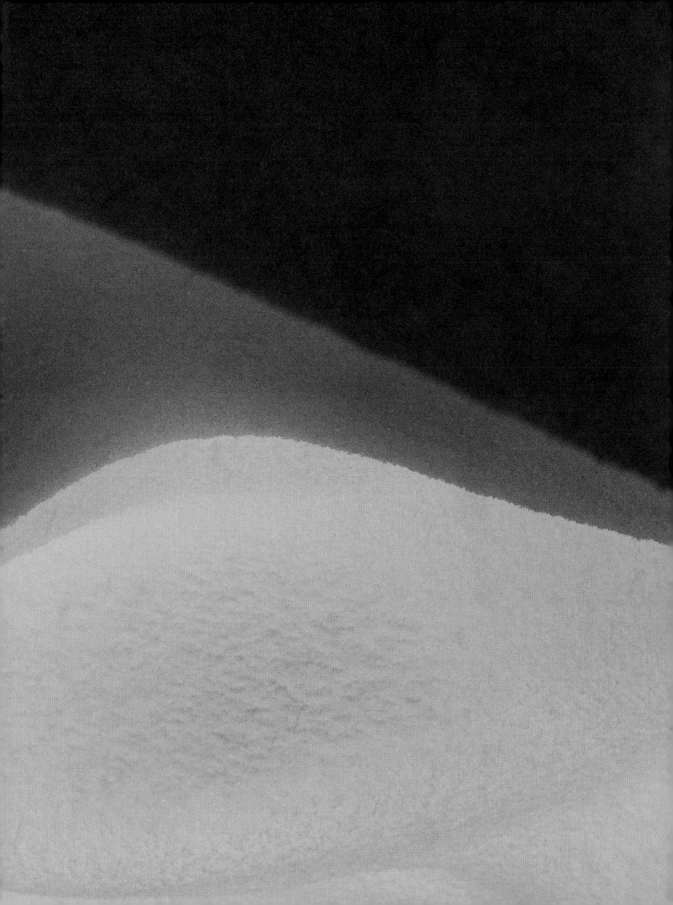

SNOW FOOD

WARMING WINTER ALPINE DISHES

LINDOR WINK

PHOTOGRAPHY: PATRIK ENGSTRÖM

Hardie Grant

BOOKS

CONTENTS

THE JOY OF FOOD AND FLUFFY POWDER

SKIING HAS BEEN close to my heart ever since early childhood. With a family obsessed with skiing, I started early and my interest in skis, snow and tall mountains grew quickly.

Apart from skiing and countless hours on the slopes, I also spent a lot of time in the cafe run by my family in Oxelösund. This is where my interest in food was born. Filled with curiosity, I observed everything going on in the kitchen and my parents realised early on that I would probably work with food later in life. And so it proved to be.

Today, I work all over the world and my goal is to let myself be inspired by wherever I currently find myself.

After culinary school I had my sights set on finding an interesting job, and that became the start of an eventful period of my life. Even at this stage, I was driven by the feeling that there was so much to discover outside of Sweden, so many things I wanted to experience, try out and be a part of. I realised at that moment that I had to grasp every opportunity and make the most of every chance I was given. After spending some time in Norway, I became interested in Åre, a ski resort in the northern Swedish mountains. That's where the skiing was …

Having arrived in Åre, I realised that I could devote myself to the things I enjoy most: cooking and first-class skiing.

I have always endeavoured to follow my dreams and to enjoy myself as much as possible along the way – which is sometimes easier said than done. During my first years as a chef, my dream was always to one day work in the top restaurants in Sweden, with the best chefs. And starting at the renowned restaurant Oaxen Krog in the Swedish archipelago, my journey continued towards the top restaurants in Stockholm. A whole new world of gastronomical adventures opened up when I was given the opportunity of working under the best chefs, all with their distinct personalities and styles of cooking. All those hours in the kitchen with Magnus Ek, Mathias Dahlgren, Adam Dahlberg and Tommy Myllymäki have given me experience, inspiration and an invaluable foundation for everything I know and practise today. I look back with pleasure on eventful years when I was given the chance to work at Sweden's best restaurants, represent Sweden in culinary contests all over the world and lead the chefs of the future to victory in the Culinary Olympics as the coach for the Junior National Culinary Team.

"Good food and snow are good for you!"

FOOD AND SKIING have been my main interests for as long as I can remember, so perhaps it's no coincidence that I combined the best of these two worlds when I lived in the Swiss mountains. Not only did I experience the best off-piste skiing in Europe, a different culture and cooking a lot of good food for skiers from all over the world, I also made fantastic new friends for life – something I value greatly. For me, food has always involved social interaction, and this is extremely important to me. Just sitting at a beautifully laid table makes me happy, it is not only the meal being served but the feeling of togetherness with my nearest and dearest that is the important thing.

In Switzerland, I had the opportunity to make new friends through good food and fluffy powder on the mountains. I got to know skiers, photographers, travel guides, colleagues, locals – people who genuinely love snow-covered mountains and eating well. What we have in common is that we live in the present and have an all-consuming passion for the things we live for. This has given me a bigger and broader perspective on life and has made me even more motivated to continue seeking new adventures and challenges in the realm where togetherness and food complement each other in the ultimate way.

When I was asked to write this book, it felt just right – of course I wanted to share some of my recipes with those who want to eat well after an active day. My cooking is, after all, about not complicating things while maintaining great taste and a sense of fun. That's why my recipes are easy for anyone to follow. I want it to be just as enjoyable and simple for you to cook as it is for me. Obviously, it may take a few minutes longer for you to complete a dish the first time you try it – like every new thing you try. Perhaps you have to read the recipe again. But when you have made it a couple of times, you will probably know it by heart and then things really take off. You might even try to develop the recipe according to your own tastes and ideas!

FOR ME IT IS important that everyone who reads this book will be inspired and feel the joy spreading through their body while cooking a meal – the same feeling you get on the first ski run of the season. Good food and snow are good for you!

LINDOR WINK

I have intentionally not included total cooking times in the recipes – everyone cooks at their own pace. So be sure to read through the recipe you want to cook beforehand and make your own estimations.

All recipes are designed for four portions. Cup measures are 250 ml (8½ fl oz), tablespoons are 15 ml (½ fl oz). Cooks using 20 ml (¾ fl oz) tablespoons should be scant with their measurements.

THE SHORTCUT TO SUCCESS

THE BEST SHORTCUT to success in the kitchen is to never skimp on the quality of your basic ingredients. The market for quality cooking in and around our popular ski resorts has grown exponentially over recent years and I can almost guarantee that local food artisans have something that will appeal to all of us, not least through the sheer quality of their basic ingredients. And yes, it will probably cost a bit more, but you will not be disappointed since it will both taste better and also benefit someone who really knows what they are doing. That's passion!

When you're on holiday you will rarely encounter a kitchen that resembles the one you are used to at home. It is therefore a good idea to, if possible, pack some of your favourite utensils for the trip. Here are my five favourites that enable me to go that extra mile.

THERMOMETER
A thermometer will help you achieve the best results with many dishes, not only meat and fish.

KNIFE
The difference between a dull and a sharp knife is comparable to that of skiing downhill with steel-edged skis and plain wooden ones. Packing a good knife is definitely worth it!

CORKSCREW
I've lost count of the number of times I've forgotten to pack my corkscrew on my way to a new location. Mine now resides permanently in my suitcase.

THERMOS
You might expect to find a thermos in all holiday homes, but it is never a sure safe bet. Pack one just in case – you never know when you might want to bring something warming with you for a day on the slopes.

MANDOLIN
If you haven't already got a mandolin it's high time to invest in one! This utensil can be used for most vegetables and I use mine all the time.

IN MY PROFESSION AS A CHEF and cook, it's all about planning. Even when I'm away I try to think and think again in order to save time. What do I need to bring along and what can I buy locally? Can I combine the menu so that the things I've taken with me can be used in several dishes?

PLAN SOME MEALS AHEAD OF TIME
- Make a shopping list.
- If you have time, prepare a couple of dinners before you travel. It's always nice to have the first meal ready planned after a day's travelling.
- Check what you already have at home before you go shopping. It's easy to pick up packs of things you already have in abundance, such as spices and coffee filters.

GOOD START

BROWN BREAKFAST BUTTER

When I started my professional life as a newly qualified chef, brown butter was something nearly everyone was talking about that I still didn't have a grip on.

There are hundreds of ways to use brown butter; here, I've mixed ordinary butter with brown butter so I can start the day with this delicacy on my breakfast sandwich.

500 g (1 lb 2 oz/2 cups) butter at
   room-temperature
salt

1. Brown half the butter in a saucepan until golden brown.

2. Take the pan off the heat to cool down.

3. Combine the brown butter with the remaining butter.

4. Add salt to taste.

Note!

Use medium heat to bring out the notes and fragrance of nutty caramel. The pan must not be too hot as the protein in the butter can easily burn at the bottom of the pan, so whisk continuously. It is the protein that provides the rich and flavourful taste.

The clever thing about brown butter is that it can be varied in so many ways. I usually flavour it with lemon, herbs or soy sauce.

Which will be your favourite?

NUT BREAD

One weekend morning at my home in Oxelösund, I was given a slice of this nut bread. It was delicious in a completely new way. It provided lasting satisfaction, not only momentarily. This recipe is one of many that follow me around the world. I have shared it with many friends, who have been spurred on to make it for themselves after trying a slice.

OVEN: 160°C (320 °F)

140 g (5 oz) dried apricots

125 g (4½ oz) almonds, blanched

50 g (1¾ oz) hazelnuts, blanched

100 g (3½ oz) walnuts

95 g (3¼ oz) linseeds (flax seeds)

75 g (2¾ oz) sunflower seeds

90 g (3 oz) pepitas (pumpkin seeds)

95 g (3¼ oz) sesame seeds

6 eggs

100 ml (3½ fl oz) canola (rapeseed) oil

1 tsp salt

1. Chop the apricots and mix with the remaining ingredients in a mixing bowl to a firm consistency.

2. Let the dough swell for 30 minutes.

3. Line a loaf tin with baking paper and add the mixture.

4. Put in the oven and bake for approx. 1 hour.

5. Remove the bread from the tin and let cool on a wire rack.

HIGH ON THE MOUNTAIN WONDERFUL CHEESE IS MADE

Engelberg has been my second home for many years. When I'm not there, I dream my way back to this village in the Swiss Alps where life is not rushed like in the big city. There is plenty of time here, and space to live in the moment, savouring all that the surroundings have to offer.

ENGELBERG HAS A rich history, with its renowned monastery – dating back to the 12th century – embedded between the snow-covered peaks. It's still a place for spiritual seekers today and a meeting place for Christian groups where the Benedictine monks sing vespers in the evening. And yet, it is not the monastery that leads people to congregate here, but the easily accessible off-piste skiing the village offers all skiing aficionados. In summer, the hiking trails and lakes are popular.

Apart from the unique opportunities offered by the mountain, there are other points of interest, even if they are not as spectacular. By the large, beautiful monastery lies the small cheese shop Shaue Käserei Kloster Engelberg. Its proprietor has a passion for both quality and service and I love to browse the well-chosen selection of tasty cheeses made from the milk of the animals that graze in the enormous meadows on the slopes of the mountains.

Despite the fact that I have spent many winters in the village, it took me a while to find out about this little local gem, probably because my interests were, first and foremost, directed towards the mountain and skiing. It wasn't until about a year had passed when a colleague at the restaurant told me about the person behind the cheese production and, spontaneously one morning before work, I was invited on a behind-the-scenes tour. During this quick visit, designed to give me an understanding of the whole process, I could see for myself the amount of work that goes into making all the different kinds of cheeses. Believe me, from now on I will enjoy every piece of cheese I eat that much more.

JUST KEEPING TRACK of all the different rooms and refrigerators we passed was difficult. To realise how many steps are involved between the cow and the cheese – from tending the animals

"Believe me, from now on I will enjoy every piece of cheese I eat that much more."

and milking, to all the steps in the manufacturing process on the premises until the cheeses are finally packaged on the store shelves – left me speechless. I remember when, a long time ago, I went on a school visit to a dairy where cheese was made. In comparison, this was on a completely different level!

THE MASTER CHEESE MAKER is the Swiss Walter Grob, a man my age who leases the monastery premises to live his dream of manufacturing and selling cheese. I do not think I have ever met a person who is so calm and composed towards his customers, although I know that his life is basically one endless work day.

Even during my first meeting with Walter, I had a clear impression of his personality and what he intends to do with his craft. His joy and passion for his chosen profession is not merely reflected in his big smile. It radiates from the enthusiastic and knowledgeable staff – in the shop as well as in the whole production process. It is apparent that everyone who works here is driven by the extreme craftsmanship needed to produce such a unique product.

After my first visit to Walter's I brought back a handful of cheese samples. Walter obviously hoped that some of them would be extra appealing to me and would be ordered for the restaurant. It wasn't difficult to choose a few favourites that my fellow chefs could use in the relatively simple and classical cooking we performed in the kitchen. Like many other Swiss restaurants, we offered our customers a cheeseboard – something that seemed sacrosanct to me in this cheese-loving country and a good way of showcasing the craftmanship of Swiss gastronomy. That the cheese is manufactured a stone's throw from the restaurant makes the whole experience all the more appealing.

The cooperation between Walter and myself – and our friendship – developed over the years in Engelberg and even if my adventures in this wonderful village are put on hold for now, I know that things are going full tilt with Walter and the gang at Shau Käserei. ❁

SPELT AND RYE CRISPBREAD

Crispbread is an old Swedish tradition that lives on today. With few ingredients, it is possible to bake a tasty bread that goes well with a variety of accompaniments and has a long shelf life. Adding spelt, rye and pepitas (pumpkin seeds) creates extra flavour.

OVEN 200°C (390 °F)

50 g (1¾ oz) spelt flour
50 g (1¾ oz) fine rye flour
100 g (3½ oz) plain (all-purpose) flour
100 ml (3½ fl oz) beer
½ tsp salt
1 tsp cooking oil
1 tbs finely chopped pepitas (pumpkin seeds)
2 tbs plain (all-purpose) flour for rolling out

1. Blend all the ingredients, apart from the 2 tbs plain flour, in a food processor over a medium speed for approx. 5 minutes.

2. Take out the dough and knead it. Cover with clingfilm and let it rest for 15 minutes.

3. Divide the dough into 4 parts and roll out each one as thinly as possible, approx. 2mm, using the 2 tbs plain flour.

4. Put the rolled-out dough on a baking sheet covered with baking paper.

5. Prick the flattened bread with a fork and bake for 8–12 minutes, until golden. Let cool on an wire rack.

A tasty crispbread is even nicer with the brown breakfast butter, see page 13.

BIRCHERMUESLI

Birchermuesli is a traditional muesli often found on the breakfast table in Switzerland. This recipe was not created by a chef but by a Swiss doctor named Bircher, who considered a nourishing diet important for his patients. The mixture is very simple to make, it lasts for a week in the fridge and, above all, keeps you feeling full for a long time, which is ideal for an active person.

160 g (5½ oz) rolled oats
300 ml (10 fl oz) coconut milk
35 g (1¼ oz) desiccated coconut
200 ml (7 fl oz) apple juice
1 tbs honey
½ tsp ground cinnamon
2 Medjool dates
2 tsp fresh grated ginger

1. Mix together the oats, coconut milk, desiccated coconut, apple juice, honey and cinnamon.

2. Chop the dates and add to the mixture.

3. Grate the ginger and squeeze out the juice. Add ginger juice to the mixture to taste.

4. Mix well and leave in the fridge overnight.

Top with berries, fruit or nuts of your choice.

GRANOLA WITH HONEY AND COCOA NIBS

Making your own granola is super simple and often ends up being more nutritious and delicious than store-bought varieties. This is an easy way to liven up your breakfast in a couple of minutes for the best possible start to the day.

OVEN: 170°C (340 °F)

125 g (4½ oz) almonds
80 g (2½ oz) oats
50 g (1¾ oz) sunflower seeds
60 g (2 oz) pepitas (pumpkin seeds)
100 g (3½ oz) runny honey
35 g (1¼ oz) desiccated coconut
50 g (1¾ oz) goji berries
50 g (1¾ oz) cocoa nibs

1. Roast the almonds, oats, sunflower seeds and pumpkin seeds in the oven on baking trays separately for 8–10 minutes.

2. Drizzle the honey over the almonds and oats and roast for a further 5–7 minutes. Let cool.

3. Mix all the roasted ingredients together, then add the coconut, goji berries and cocoa nibs.

Tastes wonderful with filmjölk (a type of Swedish soured milk), yoghurt or a bowl of milk.

Top with some extra honey.

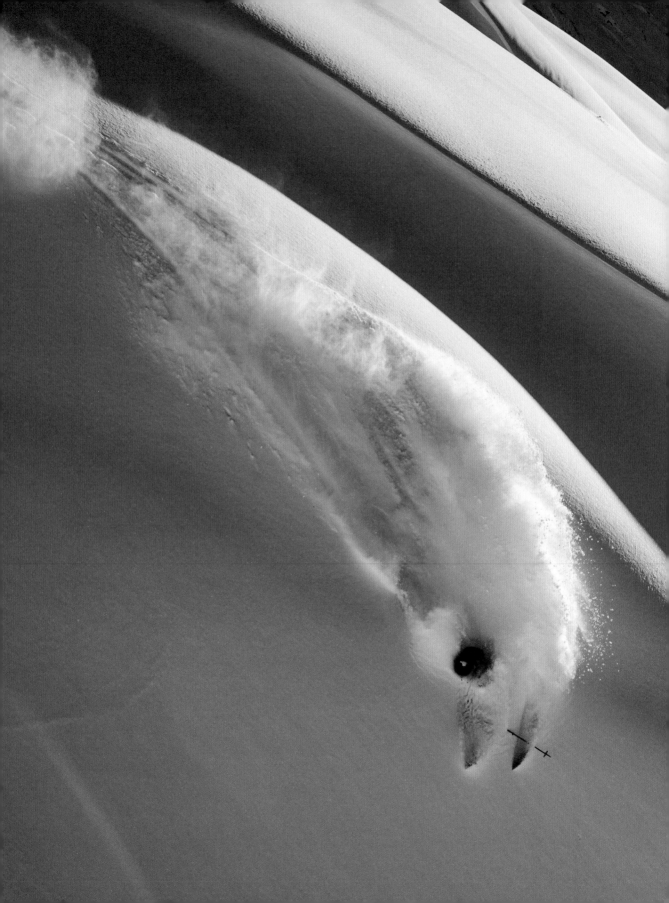

PORRIDGE WITH BUTTER-ROASTED SUNFLOWER SEEDS AND APPLE PURÉE

For long intensive days full of activities, it is important to boost your energy in the morning. Porridge may not be everyone's favourite, but when you smell the flavour of the lightly toasted sunflower seeds in the brown butter, I guarantee you will be ready to tuck in.

PORRIDGE
160 g (5½ oz) oats
900 ml (30½ fl oz) water
2 tbs linseeds (flax seeds)
½ tsp salt
50 g (1¾ oz) butter
50 g (1¾ oz) sunflower seeds

APPLE PURÉE
4 red apples
50 ml (1¾ fl oz) water
1 tbs honey
ground cardamom, to taste

PORRIDGE

1. Mix the oats, water, flaxseeds and salt in a saucepan.

2. Bring to the boil and simmer over a low heat for 4–5 minutes, stirring continuously.

3. Brown the butter (see page 13). Add the sunflower seeds and lightly toast them in the butter.

APPLE PURÉE

1. Quarter the apples and remove the core. Boil in the water until soft in a covered saucepan.

2. Remove the apple quarters and blend into a smooth purée. Add the honey and cardamom to taste.

Fill your bowl with porridge then add a generous amount of the sunflower seeds and brown butter. Top this fantastic breakfast with a large spoonful of apple purée and some cold milk.

OPEN SANDWICH WITH SCRAMBLED EGG, GRAVLAX AND SPINACH

A big breakfast is essential for those living an active life in the open air. I have always preferred more of a cooked breakfast, but I am rarely eager to cook a full-blown meal in the morning – especially if I'm in a hurry to get away for the day, which is often the case. But there are some simple ways of finding a solution – here is one of them.

6 eggs
2 tbs thick (double/heavy)
  cream
1 tbs butter
200 g (7 oz) spinach
1 tbs olive oil
fresh horseradish
1 punnet cress
4 slices rye bread
8 slices gravlax
salt, black pepper

1. Whisk together the eggs, cream and a pinch of salt.

2. Melt the butter in a saucepan over a medium heat and pour into the egg mixture.

3. Stir continuously with a spatula until the mixture starts to thicken and acquires a creamy consistency.

4. Add black pepper to taste.

5. Fry the spinach in the oil over a high heat for 1 minute. Add salt to taste.

6. Peel and grate the horseradish and cut the cress with scissors.

To make the sandwiches: start with the bread, add the spinach, then the eggs and finally the gravlax. Top with the cress and freshly grated horseradish.

BRING ALONG

CELERIAC AND SWEDE SOUP WITH TOASTED SEEDS

Soups of every kind remind me of my childhood and are therefore always close to my heart. Since I was a kid they have been there, either on the table or as a packed lunch stored in a thermos. If you ask me, a warm soup and a sandwich is the optimal ski lunch when you want to fit in a few extra runs.

½ celeriac

½ swede (rutabaga)

2 carrots

1 leek

200 ml (7 fl oz) double (thick) cream

1 vegetable stock cube (10 g/ ¼ oz) + 300 ml (10 fl oz) water

3 tbs pepitas (pumpkin seeds)

3 tbs sunflower seeds

salt

a good handful parsley

1. Peel the root vegetables and cut into pieces.

2. Slice the leeks lengthways, rinse off any dirt and cut into pieces.

3. Bring the water and cream to the boil with the stock cube, then add the root vegetables and leek. Boil until soft.

4. Blend the soup until smooth and add salt to taste.

5. Toast the pumpkin and sunflower seeds with a little salt in a dry frying pan.

6. Chop the parsley.

7. Serve the soup with a sprinkle of seeds and parsley on top.

VICHYSSOISE WITH KALE

Soups are sometimes forgotten in the home kitchen but are nearly always available at restaurants in ski resorts. It is easy to understand why: a warming and tasty soup can be exactly what you need after a long day in the cold. Here is a classic with a new twist.

1 leek
100 g (3½ oz) kale, stems
   removed
1 garlic clove
1 tbs olive oil
200 g (7 oz) potatoes
1 litre (34 fl oz/4 cups) water
200 ml (7 fl oz) double
   (thick) cream
2 vegetable stock cubes
   (20 g/¾ oz)
salt, black pepper
200 g (7 oz) cooked
   chickpeas, to serve
a handful parsley, to serve

1. Chop the leek, kale and garlic. Fry in the oil until the kale has collapsed and the leek starts to soften.

2. Peel and dice the potatoes and add to the pan with the water, cream and stock cubes.

3. Let everything simmer until the potatoes are soft.

4. Blend the soup, then add salt and black pepper to taste.

5. Serve with the chickpeas and chopped parsley.

SPICY CARROT SOUP WITH CRISPY BACON

A spicy and warming carrot soup is quick and easy to make. Why not prepare it the day before and take it with you to the slopes?

500 g (1 lb 2 oz) carrots

1 onion

1 garlic clove

2 tbs olive oil

1 tsp ground cumin

2 tbs grated ginger

¼ tsp chilli flakes

400 ml (13½ fl oz) coconut milk

400 ml (13½ fl oz) water

1 chicken or vegetable stock cube (10 g/¼ oz)

½ tsp salt

2 tbs fresh lime juice

150 g (5½ oz) bacon rashers

a handful flat-leaf (Italian) parsley

1. Slice the carrots, onions and garlic. Fry in a saucepan with the oil, cumin, ginger and chilli flakes until everything takes on a bit of colour.

2. Add the coconut milk, water and stock cube.

3. Simmer without a lid until the carrots are soft, approx. 15–20 minutes.

4. Blend the soup until smooth and add the salt and lime juice to taste.

5. Cut the bacon into pieces and fry until crispy.

6. Serve the soup with the bacon and finely chopped parsley.

SEED BARS

You will be able to throw these delicious and energy-providing seed bars together in a jiffy – they are ideal to bring along as a quick snack.

5 Medjool dates
10 dried apricots
2 tbs cold coffee
55 g (2 oz) hazelnuts
60 g (2 oz) blanched almonds
4 tbs oats
2 tbs sesame seeds
1 tbs peanut butter
2 tbs olive oil

1. Remove the stones from the dates and soak them in the coffee, together with the apricots.

2. Blend or finely chop the nuts and almonds, then combine with the oats and sesame seeds.

3. Blend the dates, apricots and coffee with the peanut butter and olive oil.

4. Fold into the nut and seed mixture to form an even dough.

5. Flatten the dough between 2 baking sheets and put it into the fridge for 1 hour.

6. Cut into 12 individual portions.

SOFT FLATBREAD ROLLS WITH SAUERKRAUT

Central Europe does not only offer high mountains and fantastic skiing, it's also known for its sausages and their accompaniments. One of my favourite side dishes is sauerkraut. It's also easy to pack a few sausages and some soft flatbread in your backpack.

If you can't cook the sausages on site, cook them at home and bring them along in a thermos.

1 can of sauerkraut (300 g/ 10½ oz)
4 crushed juniper berries
1 tsp caraway seeds
8 Frankfurt sausages
2 bay leaves
3 allspice berries
4 soft flatbreads
mustard, to taste

1. In a bowl, mix the sauerkraut with the juniper berries and caraway seeds. Put them into a sealed container.

2. Heat the sausages in boiling water with the bay leaf and allspice and place in a thermos.

3. Pack the sauerkraut, sausages, flatbread and mustard – and lunch is ready as soon as you get hungry.

ROSEHIP SOUP

Simple, tasty and nutritious. Bring a thermos to the slopes or top up your energy levels with a cup of this as a snack at home in your chalet. Cold or warm – it's your choice!

1 litre (34 fl oz/4 cups) water
70 g (2½ oz) rosehip flour
3 tbs unrefined sugar or honey
1 tbs potato flour

1. Pour the water into a saucepan and whisk in the dry ingredients.
2. Bring to the boil, stirring constantly, and hey presto, it's ready.

BRINGING THE FLATBREAD TRADITION INTO THE PRESENT DAY

Fine traditions and culinary craftsmanship should be preserved and maintained. But how do you avoid the "that's the way we've always done it" trap of being conservationist rather than someone who carries the craft forward into the present day and beyond?

I AM IN ÅRE in Jämtland, the centre of Sweden's alpine skiing. I have spent a lot of time here in the mountains ever since I was a child: first with my family and, later, in the winters, working for various restaurants. This is an area that teems with entrepreneurship. There are many driving forces who administrate and develop Jämtland's culinary heritage.

I am looking for someone who can show me how to bake soft flatbread the traditional way. Many people might associate soft flatbread with a Swedish fast food classic: tunnbrödsrulle. Frankfurters with mashed potato and a prawn salad rolled up in a piece of flatbread and wolfed down on the way home after a long evening. For me, a flatbread roll should contain reindeer meat and be eaten on a day on the slopes – a classic. Served with a thermos of hot cocoa and life could not get better!

RUMOURS LEAD US to the Åre Heritage Centre, where Sofia Carlsson has recently taken over the management. It is late autumn when photographer Patrik and I visit Sofia, and the first signs of snow are in the air. The Heritage Centre is on the outskirts of the village, in a beautiful

"She wants to honour the rich heritage but still develop the site into a vibrant meeting place."

valley bordering the Ullån River, with a view over the Åreskuta mountains to the east and the Snasahögarna mountain range to the west, a popular area for tourist skiing.

Sofia is full of plans for what she wants to achieve with the Heritage Centre. She wants to honour the rich heritage but still develop the site into a vibrant meeting place. The Heritage Centre itself consists of a main house, two buildings that were used for food storage and supplies and a barn that houses a baking oven, a loft and a smithy. In one of the buildings, she now runs a cafe and a small museum where you can see what life was like in a mountain farm homestead during the 19th century.

INSIDE THE CAFE the fire is crackling and selected books are placed around the room for inspiration. Many deal with permaculture (a design principle for sustainable cultivation), which Sofia avidly supports. The key words for the entire enterprise are sustainability and ecology. When you enter this place it is like a journey back in time that corresponds with my experience of how life is led in the mountains and the Alps, maintaining and living with old traditions while integrating them into the modern world. It provides calm, pride and joy on a small scale with many disparate participants. Both then and now.

The oven chimney billows smoke, the chickens are pecking in the yard and by the baking house stands a mountain of roughly hewn logs that have to be brought in before the baking can start. We lug logs and fire up the oven. Sofia prepares the dough and while it rises, she serves coffee and a flatbread roll with reindeer meat.

The soft flatbread is baked in a wood-fired oven. The wood is mainly birch and aspen and the temperature is high – up to 400°C (750°F). Sofia seems to go by feel and she senses when the temperature is right. She then rakes the embers towards the side and back walls of the oven.

The fire is intense and beautiful and Patrik keeps snapping away with his camera while Sofia quickly divides the dough into even round balls – still working by feel and routine. No scales for her. Confidently, she starts to roll out the dough. I try to keep track of her actions as best I can. She is a brilliant and entertaining baking teacher and, like so many others I have met up here, you have to

"walk the talk". There is no tolerance of bullshit, you have to show what you're made of through your actions.

First she flours the baking table, where she has covered the wood with a soft cloth. Then she rolls out the small balls of dough into large sheets, all of them the same size, using a striated rolling pin for even and smooth rolling. Easier said than done, I realise, when trying to keep up with Sofia.

Before the bread goes into the oven, she rolls it again with a notched rolling pin to ensure even baking. When I've managed to make one I consider even and perfectly round, and Sofia has approved it, it's time to carefully lift it onto a baking peel using a baking stick and quickly transferring it into the red-hot oven. You place the bread straight onto the baking stone, more or less in and out again – not a moment longer than ten seconds.

We bake about forty flatbreads, the daily requirement of the cafe, and finish with a couple that we munch straight out of the oven. After the morning's work, it is a rich reward to eat warm flatbread with butter. A delicacy in its simplicity, melting in the mouth.

I'm so inspired by meeting and baking with Sofia and by her passion. At the same time, I feel a profound humility. It's so easy to forget the totality, the work that underlies our Swedish culinary heritage. Given that few of us have a wood-fired oven at home, I try to bake a flatbread that does not require one when I return home. The recipe can be found on page 70. ✽

ABOUT SOFT FLATBREAD

Flatbread has been baked in Sweden since the 16th century. It was primarily used as a method of preservation, as seed husks contain fat and therefore tend to go rancid more quickly. Drying and baking into bread extended the grain's shelf life. As a consequence, large quantities of flatbread were baked and stored in big barrels.

Barley was the grain used and that is why we connect flatbread with Norrland in the north of Sweden; barley was the grain that was easiest to cultivate and hardiest in the north. In times of food shortages, the dough was stretched by adding bark.

The flatbread in those days was quite different to the flatbread we are used to today, which is usually baked with wheat, with the occasional addition of rye.

Exotic? Well ... Indian chapatis and naan, Mexican tortillas, pitta bread and even pizza are baked in a similar way.

STEAK SANDWICH WITH CURRY MAYONNAISE AND PICKLE

I consider a substantial lunch to be the obvious choice. A filling sandwich in your backpack is a simple way of taming your hunger.

Here I fill a baguette with thinly sliced steak, lettuce, pickle and curry mayonnaise. The steak can, of course, be substituted with something else. Perhaps some leftovers from yesterday's dinner?

2 slices steak (approx. 100 g/ 3½ oz per person)
3 tbs olive oil
1 onion
1 tbs butter
1 tsp curry powder
300 ml (10 fl oz) mayonnaise
½ tsp dijon mustard
20 cornichons
1 shallot
2 baguettes
1 head of lettuce
salt, black pepper

1. Pepper and salt the steaks. Fry them in the oil over a high heat for approx. 2 minutes per side. Let them rest for a few minutes after frying.

2. Peel and finely chop the onion, then sauté it in the butter and curry powder until soft. Let cool.

3. Combine the onion with the mayonnaise and mustard and add salt to taste.

4. Cut the cornichons lengthways.

5. Peel and thinly slice the shallot.

6. Slice the steaks into thin strips.

7. Cut the baguettes in 2, then cut each part lengthways, but not all the way through.

8. Spread the curry mayonnaise on the bread.

9. Add plenty of lettuce, then place the steak on top.

10. Top with curry mayonnaise, cornichons and the sliced onion.

That's lunch taken care of!

WINTERY VEGETABLE SOUP

You can't always count on there being a restaurant nearby when you are skiing. Here is a suggestion for something that is easy and filling. Cook it outdoors or bring it along with you in a thermos.

2 onions
2 garlic cloves
2 tbs olive oil
2 sprigs of thyme
3 carrots
200 g (7 oz) potatoes of a waxy variety
½ head of Savoy cabbage
1 litre (34 fl oz/4 cups) water
2 chicken or vegetable stock cubes (20 g/¾ oz)
salt, black pepper

1. Peel and thinly slice the onions and garlic.

2. Heat the oil in a saucepan and fry the onions, garlic and thyme over a medium heat until the onions are soft and translucent, making sure they do not brown.

3. Meanwhile, slice the carrots, potatoes and cabbage to equal size.

4. Add the carrots and potatoes to the saucepan and cook for a further minute or two.

5. Pour in the water and bring to the boil. Add the stock cubes and simmer until the vegetables are soft. Take out the thyme sprigs. Just before serving, stir in the cabbage and give the soup a final, quick boil, adding salt to taste.

BACK HOME

MUSHROOM CROQUETTES WITH PARSLEY AND GARLIC

When you just want to sit back and relax, few things stimulate the taste buds like freshly fried croquettes. With their crunchy exteriors and flavourful, piping hot interiors, beer has found its ideal accompaniment. Enjoy.

200 g (7 oz) potatoes
1 onion
1 garlic clove
50 g (1¾ oz) butter
150 g (5½ oz) button mushrooms
1 tbs olive oil
1 tbs crème fraîche
a good handful parsley
juice and zest of 1 lemon
2 tbs plain (all-purpose) flour
2 beaten eggs
120 g (4½ oz) breadcrumbs
500 ml (17 fl oz/2 cups) oil for frying
salt

1. Peel and boil the potatoes until soft.

2. Peel and finely chop the onion and garlic. Brown the onion and garlic in half the butter until soft and golden brown.

3. Slice the mushrooms. Add salt and fry in the olive oil and remaining butter.

4. Mash the potatoes with a fork and stir in the onion and garlic, mushrooms and crème fraîche.

5. Chop and add the parsley and half the lemon zest. Add lemon juice and salt to taste.

6. Shape the mixture into 16 small balls. Roll the balls in the flour, dip into the beaten egg and cover in breadcrumbs.

7. Heat the oil to 200°C (390 °F) in a heavy-bottomed saucepan (use a thermometer) and fry the croquettes until golden brown.

Note!

Remember that deep-frying splashes oil, so use a deep saucepan and never fill the oil to more than a third of the way up.

(The croquettes are pictured to the right of the beverages in the photo opposite.)

CRISPY ONION WITH A CAPER AND TARRAGON DIP

Deep-fried foods of all kind are usually popular in most households. After a day filled with activities, the craving for salt is often huge. These bread-fried onions may sound a bit mundane but the sweetness of the onions after cooking, combined with the salty crispiness of the batter will not disappoint. Enjoy with a glass of cold beer.

CAPER AND TARRAGON DIP
1 egg yolk
1 tsp dijon mustard
1 tbs vinegar
300 ml (10 fl oz) cooking oil
1 tbs capers
handful fresh tarragon
salt

CRISPY ONION
60 g (2 oz) coarse rye flour
30 g (1 oz) plain (all-purpose) flour
200 ml (7 fl oz) beer
¼ tsp salt
4 large shallots
1 litre (34 fl oz/4 cups) cooking oil

DIP

1. Whisk the egg yolk, mustard and vinegar together.

2. Add the oil, drop by drop at first and then in a slow trickle, whisking continuously.

3. Add salt to taste.

4. Finely chop the capers and tarragon, then fold into the mayonnaise.

ONION

1. Whisk together the rye flour, plain flour, beer and salt.

2. Peel and cut the shallots into long narrow pieces.

3. Put the shallots into the flour mixture batter and toss and turn them until coated.

4. Heat the oil to 180°C (360 °F) in a heavy-bottomed saucepan (use a thermometer).

5. Lift the onion pieces from the batter and fry until golden brown and crispy. Dry the onions on a kitchen towel before serving.

Serve the onions with the dip.

Note!
Strain and save the oil when it has cooled – you never know when it's frying time again!

ENDIVE SALAD WITH BLUE CHEESE AND ORANGE

I can see a trend in both the Swedish and the European mountains: small local producers are becoming more and more common. Or perhaps I am just suddenly more aware of them ...

During my years in Engelberg, I came into contact with the local butchers as well as one of the village's cheese producers, a Swiss contemporary of mine named Walter. He manufactures and sells the best cheese in the village. Thanks to Walter I have acquired a whole new appreciation for those who work with passion on their personal interests, something I also recognise in myself.

2 endives
2 oranges
3 tbs olive oil
2 slices rye bread
2 tbs butter
100 g (3½ oz) blue cheese
salt, black pepper
nasturtium leaves, to serve

1. Trim the root from the endive so the leaves fall apart.

2. Peel the oranges with a sharp knife and then fillet the segments from the membranes. Collect the juice (see page 98).

3. Mix the orange juice with the olive oil. Add salt and pepper to taste.

4. Dice the rye bread into approx. 1 × 1 cm (½ × ½ in) bread cubes and fry them in the butter over a medium heat until crispy.

5. Arrange the endive leaves and the orange segments on 4 plates. Add the rye bread croutons and crumble the blue cheese over the top.

6. Drizzle with plenty of the orange and olive oil dressing.

RADISHES WITH A DIP OF CHICKPEAS AND WHITE BEANS

I've always liked beans and peas in all their forms. It's only now, during my years competing in culinary contests and being leader of the Swedish Junior Chefs National Team, that I have started collaborating with producers who work with these ingredients and have gained a new insight into the wide range of uses they provide. I now regularly buy these products and use them in my everyday cooking.

Here is a quick snack that only takes a few minutes to conjure up.

2 bunches radishes

1 bunch carrots

150 g (5½ oz) cooked white beans

150 g (5½ oz) cooked chickpeas

1 garlic clove

100 ml (3½ fl oz) olive oil

juice of 1 lemon

paprika powder, to taste

toasted sesame seeds

salt

1. Trim and rinse the radishes and carrots.

2. Rinse the beans and chickpeas thoroughly.

3. Blend the beans and chickpeas with the garlic and olive oil. If you like, add a little water for a smoother consistency.

4. Add lemon juice, paprika and salt to taste.

5. Sprinkle with the sesame seeds.

SOFT FLATBREAD WITH REINDEER HEART AND HORSERADISH

No one who has travelled to the north of Sweden can have missed the Swedish "Renklämma" – the reindeer roll. An early memory of mine is when my family visited a Same village and were offered thinly sliced reindeer meat on a buttered piece of soft flatbread. It felt luxurious sitting there on the reindeer furs in the crispy cold air in the "kåta", which is a Sami teepee. A little taste of another culture.

FLATBREAD

200 ml (7 fl oz) milk

25 g (1 oz) yeast, fresh

2 tbs treacle

2 tbs butter at room
    temperature

180 g (6½ oz) plain
    (all-purpose) flour

120 g (4½ oz) rye flour

½ tsp salt

TOPPING

200 g (7 oz) sliced smoked
    reindeer heart, or other
    venison, preferably smoked

200 g (7 oz) sour cream

fresh horseradish, grated or
    ready-grated horseradish,
    to taste

a good handful chives

salt, black pepper

SOFT FLATBREAD

1. Mix all the flatbread ingredients together and knead into a firm dough.

2. Let the dough rise in the fridge for 30 minutes.

3. Divide the dough into 16 round balls and roll them flat, approx. 3mm (⅛ in).

4. Prick the flatbreads with a fork and fry them quickly on both sides in a hot, dry frying pan.

TOPPING

1. Grate the horseradish and mix with the sour cream to your taste. Add salt and black pepper to taste.

2. Top the flatbreads with the reindeer heart, the horseradish and sour cream mixture and garnish with chopped chives.

Note!

If you can't find reindeer heart, elk heart makes a fine substitute.

TARTE FLAMBÉE WITH FRIED ONION AND BLACK CABBAGE

During the time I worked at Mathias Dahlgren's restaurants, I learned to work with simple ingredients in a completely new way. Due to his clear food philosophy and with the approach of "less is more", I suddenly understood the greatness of cooking ingredients to perfection in a relatively simple yet luxurious way. It has been of tremendous importance to me on my journey as a chef into the world.

OVEN: BASES 150°C (300°F), TOPPING 210°C (410°F)

——

BASES (ordinary pizza dough works as well)
240 g (8½ fl oz) plain (all-purpose) flour
½ tsp baking powder
⅓ tsp salt
100 ml (3½ fl oz) water
2 tbs olive oil

TOPPING
3 onions
cooking oil for frying
1 bunch black cabbage
1 garlic clove
300 g (10½ oz) smetana (sour cream)
50 g (1¾ oz) parmesan
a good handful parsley
juice of ½ lemon
salt, black pepper

BASES

1. Mix all the ingredients together and knead into a supple dough. Let it rest in the fridge for 10 minutes.

2. Divide the dough into 4 pieces and roll out as thinly as possible on a lightly floured work surface. Prick with a fork.

3. Bake the bases on a baking sheet covered with baking paper for 25–30 minutes.

TOPPING

1. Peel and slice the onions. Fry in oil until soft and golden. Add salt and pepper to taste.

2. Shred the black cabbage and fry it in a little oil for approx. 1 minute. Add the grated garlic.

3. Spread the smetana on the baked bases and grate parmesan on top. Cover with the onions and black cabbage.

4. Bake the tarts for approx. 5 minutes.

5. Top with the chopped parsley, black pepper and lemon juice.

POWDER – THEN AN IPA, AND ANOTHER ONE TO KEEP IT COMPANY

After a long and glorious day on the slopes, a bit tired but totally content, nothing beats a cold beer – preferably accompanied by a bite of something salty, maybe something deep fried ...

WE ARE IN CHAMONIX, the iconic French ski resort area in the Haute-Savoie region. The village is situated at the foot of the Mont Blanc Massif, with its eleven separate peaks, each reaching more than 4000 metres (13123 feet) above sea level. Here you will find some of Europe's largest glaciers and the most impressive vertical drops you can encounter for skiing.

Chamonix is also the setting for innumerable anecdotes and tall tales about heroic and mock-heroic exploits on the mountain. Some of the most fanciful stories are those that Patrik, the photographer, tries to tell me about Françoise, the mountain guide who, in the 1980s, planned to roll down the side of the 4810 metre (13713 feet) Mont Blanc inside a gigantic plastic ball. And the one about the big jacuzzi party held at the top of the mountain in 2007.

But apart from the odd lunatic, this little village attracts the most accomplished and famous figures in skiing, mountaineering, climbing and trail running. Passion is the word that best describes the character of the village and its inhabitants.

Foodwise, I can't stop myself from rubbing my hands with glee at the thought of eating and drinking here again, due to the fantastic quality of the primary produce and the way it is handled here. Many people in Chamonix are experts at maintaining and improving the traditional culinary heritage.

HERE IN THE MOUNTAINS, climate change is not an abstract concept but a reality that is all too intrusive. The melting glaciers are painful reminders of rising temperatures, and the changing conditions they bring affect the lives of many in the valley. Enterprises and local production that are seasonal and sustainable are therefore the obvious choice for most of the people I come into contact with.

The fact that there are no less than 300 microbreweries in the region of Haute-Savoie alone sparks my curiosity. The water from the glaciers

"I realise immediately that I have found a kindred spirit when it comes to giving one hundred per cent in everything one does."

appears to be worth its weight in gold, and a steady stream of beer trickles down a lot of thirsty throats! When I told people about my desire to meet the people who deal with culinary craftsmanship and who share my love of the mountains and skiing, preferably someone who makes beer, I was directed to Jack Gerald, a British mountaineer and mountain guide who lives in Chamonix.

The absence of – in his opinion – "good beer" led Jack to brew beer for himself and his friends in his garage. His circle of friends quickly expanded, and the garage was exchanged for larger premises in Passy, a 20 minute drive down the valley. The beer now aptly goes by the name of Big Mountain Brewing.

I realise immediately that I have found a kindred spirit when it comes to giving one hundred per cent in everything one does. Jack energetically buzzes around, checking temperatures in one place and fermentation in another. I try to keep up as best I can – this is a man in perpetual motion, whether he is on the mountain or by the spigots. The small climbing wall in the attic beside the office hints at him being able to keep busy even in his lunch hour!

Jack tells me that, after many years in the mountains, he is now ready for a new challenge and – as I have mentioned – he tackles everything he does with great energy. This has resulted in an impressive menu of really good beers, with everything from a summery, fruity NEIPA with notes of passion fruit, to a robust coffee and chocolate-tinged stout that goes under the name of Breakfast Stout, which in my opinion is better savoured in front of a crackling fire after a day of skiing than as a breakfast tipple.

No artificial additives, no added sugar, brewed with care. It is instantly recognisable by the pure, clean taste. Jack's high ambitions made him decide to get in touch with some highly skilled brewers. The French have a strong reputation for producing magnificent wines, but when it comes to beer, the best brewers come from England. In fulfilling his ambition to produce irresistible beer, Jack now has the assistance of a master brewer and two other brewers.

I LIKE THE CRAFTSMANSHIP of beer making and, as much as I like the beer, I like the underlying philosophy: clean water, no additives, recyclable beer kegs, using as much renewable energy as

possible, malt that is reintroduced to the cycle by being fed to the animals or composted, and the decision to use only electric vehicles for transportation. This goes hand in hand with how we relate to the mountains, with playfulness and humility towards our natural surroundings.

I TRAVEL BACK through the valley, up towards the small bubble of Chamonix. Instead of brewing and selling the beer from the premises, Jack and his crew run a small bar in the centre of the village. Here, you can enjoy a beer and some tasty charcuteries, cheeses or a pizza. You can also buy the beer to take home in refillable, specially constructed containers that keep the beer fresh for up to two weeks. When you've finished the beer, you just rinse the container and it's ready to be refilled. Bringing reusable containers and buying by weight or volume in order to cut transport emissions and waste through packaging is a trend that's growing in France at the moment. You can even buy your beer in the same way here. I like that.

I stay on in the bar; there are so many beers that sound yummy that I want to try – and I would like to add that the bar is situated on the main street of Chamonix which, in the afternoons, offers a parade of exciting characters who have all been on adventures in the mountains. Last but not least, you obviously want to tell your neighbours at the bar about your own incredible runs in bottomless powder snow.

With one IPA down, a NEIPA to keep it company and some good charcuterie and cheese in your stomach, I can only say that local, small scale and cyclic, in combination with a pair of skis, is the bee's knees. ❄

FRIED CHICKEN HEARTS WITH CHERRIES AND PISTACHIO NUTS

Chicken is one of the most common meats but how many people have actually tasted chicken hearts? Fried at high temperature and accompanied by sweet fruit, nuts and a buttery glaze, I can guarantee a pleasant surprise! This quick, small dish is perfect to share while waiting for dinner to finish cooking.

100 g (3½ oz) cherries
   (or bigarreau cherries)
200 g (7 oz) chicken hearts
1 tbs olive oil
50 ml (1¾ fl oz) port
1 tbs butter
1 tbs pistachio kernels
salt
watercress (optional)

1. Halve the cherries and remove the stones.

2. Trim the chicken hearts to remove any fat or membranes.

3. Salt and fry the hearts in oil over a high heat for approx. 2–3 minutes.

4. Add the port and butter and quickly reduce.

5. Cut the hearts in half and serve immediately with the cherries and pistachios. Decorate with watercress if available.

FRIED SPRING ONIONS WITH ROASTED PEPPER AND ALMONDS

When guests find their way into the kitchen asking what that heavenly smell is, I know I'm on the right track. The smell of things roasting on a barbecue is unbeatable, but you seldom have access to an outdoor barbecue in the wintertime. You have to compromise and heat a frying pan to a really high temperature. Spring onions fried at high temperature for dipping in a roasted pepper purée is the best choice for a "green" after-ski meal.

OVEN: 225°C (435°F)

1 onion
1 small garlic clove
3 red capsicums (bell peppers)
3 tbs olive oil
30 g (1 oz) blanched toasted almonds
1 tsp red wine vinegar
2 bunches spring onions (scallions)
cooking oil for frying
salt, black pepper

1. Peel the onion and garlic. Slice the onion into large segments and crush the garlic.

2. Place the onion in an ovenproof dish with the capsicums and drizzle over 1 tbs of the olive oil.

3. Roast the onions and capsicums in the oven until soft, approx. 10 minutes, and let cool.

4. Peel the peppers and remove the seeds and membranes.

5. Blend the roasted vegetables with the almonds and some olive oil to a creamy consistency. Add vinegar, salt and black pepper to taste.

6. Trim and rinse the spring onions, leaving them whole. Place on kitchen towel and leave to dry.

7. Fry the spring onions in a little cooking oil and salt, approx. 2 minutes each side.

Serve the spring onions whole, as freshly fried as possible, together with the creamed peppers – and why not with a cold, light lager or a glass of white wine with a slightly sweeter character.

CRISPY FRIED CHICKEN WITH CHILLI AND GARLIC DIP

Few things complement a cold beer as well as something deep-fried with a flavourful dip. To really spice up an after-ski, I flavour the dip with chilli, garlic and pickled jalapeño.

FRIED CHICKEN

400 g (14 oz) chicken breast

2 eggs

60 g (2 oz) plain (all-purpose) flour

50 g (1¾ oz) Panko or breadcrumbs

500 ml (17 fl oz/2 cups) cooking oil

salt

DIP

2 jalapeños

1 red chilli

a good handful coriander

1 garlic clove

200 ml (7 oz) mayonnaise

juice and zest of ½ a lime

salt

CHICKEN

1. Cut the chicken into equal pieces, approx. 2 × 2 cm (¾ × ¾ in).

2. Whisk the eggs.

3. Coat the chicken pieces in the flour, then the egg and finally the Panko.

4. Heat the oil in a saucepan to 180°C (360 °F; use a thermometer) and fry the chicken pieces until golden brown. This takes about 4–5 minutes.

5. Remove the chicken pieces and let them drain on a plate with paper towel. Add salt to taste.

DIP

1. Chop the jalapeño, chilli, coriander and garlic. Fold into the mayonnaise.

2. Add the lime juice and zest.

3. Add a pinch of salt. Serve the chicken with the dip.

Note!

When frying in a saucepan the temperature often drops quickly when you add whatever you are frying. Therefore, it's a good idea to use a thermometer while you are frying, so you can easily adjust and keep the right heat during the cooking process.

GLÜHWEIN

Glühwein is at its best sipped in front of a fire with your skiing clothes still on. You can also make a non-alcoholic alternative – I use a good apple juice instead of wine.

600 ml (20½ fl oz) red wine
100 ml (3½ fl oz) water
1 orange in pieces
2 star anise
1 cinnamon stick
1 tbs chopped ginger
175 g (6 oz) sugar
2 bay leaves
4 cloves

1. Heat all the ingredients and leave to infuse off the heat for 30 minutes.

2. Remove the spices, heat up again and serve in cups or glasses.

TOASTED SOURDOUGH BREAD WITH BURRATA AND TOMATO

It is no secret that the Italians know about simple and tasty food. Everything hinges on their respect for and quality of the ingredients. Burrata is an Italian cow's milk cheese made from mozzarella and cream. The outer layer is a firmer cheese, while the inside contains stracciatella and cream, which gives it an unusual and soft consistency. Semi-dry a few flavourful tomatoes, toast a couple of slices of sourdough bread and eat with the highest quality burrata – a very simple and filling snack.

OVEN: 140°C (285°F)

4 tomatoes
1 garlic clove
2 tbs olive oil
4 slices sourdough bread
approx. 500 g (1 lb 2 oz)
   burrata (2 pieces)
a good handful basil
flaked sea salt, black pepper

1. Cut the tomatoes into wedges and place on a baking tray lined with baking paper. Add salt and pepper.

2. Dry the tomatoes in the oven for 1½–2 hours. Open the oven door to let out steam a few times during the drying.

3. Grate the garlic and blend with olive oil. Brush the bread slices with the mixture and fry them in a frying pan over a medium heat until golden.

4. Place the tomatoes and burrata on the toast and garnish with basil.

5. Top with a couple of turns of the pepper mill and some flaked sea salt.

GET IT TOGETHER

ROASTED BEETS WITH HOLLANDAISE AND HAZELNUTS

Working around the world in different places and with chefs from different cultures is the best way to develop in my profession. This particular dish was cooked by my colleagues and me during my time in Engelberg in Switzerland, at a farewell dinner for some of the local luminaries of the skiing community. The theme was vegetarian, and the dish quickly became a firm favourite.

OVEN: 180°C (360°F)

800 g (1 lb 12 oz) beetroot
1 tbs cooking oil
55 g (2 oz) hazelnuts
200 g (7 oz) butter
3 egg yolks
2 tbs water
1 tbs pressed lemon juice
salt
a good handful thyme

1. Peel and cut the beets into wedges. Put them into an ovenproof dish.

2. Drizzle the oil over the beets and add salt. Roast in the oven for about 30–40 minutes or until the beets are soft.

3. Roast the hazelnuts in the oven for 8–10 minutes.

4. Melt the butter in a saucepan and warm to approx. 60°C (140 °F).

5. Whisk the egg yolks, water and lemon juice in another saucepan over a low heat until the mixture thickens.

6. Add the melted butter in a thin stream while whisking continuously until the sauce thickens and all the butter is added. Make sure not to use the white dregs at the bottom.

7. Add salt to taste. Place the beets onto 4 plates and pour over the hollandaise. Top with the roasted hazelnuts and sprigs of thyme.

SOCCA WITH COURGETTES AND FETA CHEESE

Socca is something new to me. Despite all my years as a chef and visits to many gastronomical cultures, I must have let this French chickpea pancake pass me by. But now it's even made me like pancakes again and maybe that's because they are usually served with savoury accompaniments. Instead of sugar and jam, the freshly made chickpea pancake is served with a variety of vegetables. My favourites are courgettes (zucchini) and aubergine (eggplant).

OVEN: 180°C (390°F)

350 g (12½ oz) chickpea flour
300 ml (10 fl oz) water
2 tbs olive oil
½ tsp bicarbonate of soda
½ tsp salt
1 aubergine (eggplant)
2 tbs olive oil
1 tsp tamari
1 tsp white wine vinegar
1 garlic clove
1 courgette (zucchini)
cooking oil for frying
100 g (3½ oz) feta cheese
1 punnet cress
freshly pressed lemon juice
salt, black pepper

1. Combine the chickpea flour, water, olive oil, bicarbonate of soda and salt into a batter. Let the batter rest in the fridge for 15 minutes.

2. Cut the aubergine lengthways and place the halves in an ovenproof dish.

3. Drizzle the olive oil over the aubergine, then add the salt and pepper.

4. Roast the aubergine in the oven until completely soft. Scoop out the contents into a bowl and add the soy and white vinegar. Press in the garlic and add a little salt to taste.

5. Cut the courgette into cubes and fry over a high heat in a little olive oil. Add some salt and black pepper.

6. Fry the pancakes in cooking oil for 2–3 minutes on each side.

7. Serve the socca with the aubergines and the fried courgettes. Crumble over the feta cheese. Top with the cut cress and a few drops of lemon juice.

SALAD OF CELERIAC, FIGS AND GRAPEFRUIT

Sour, sweet, salty and bitter. These are four of our basic senses of taste and I often use them when I think about and cook food. In this starter salad, the sweetness of the fruit meets the saltiness of the cheese, the bitterness of the olive oil and the refreshing acidity of the grapefruit. A little bit of everything in every bite!

OVEN: 200°C (390°F)

1 celeriac
1 celery stalk
4 fresh figs
2 grapefruits
1 shallot
100 ml (3½ fl oz) olive oil
4 tbs red wine vinegar
100 g (3½ oz) chèvre (goat's cheese)
1 punnet cress
salt, black pepper

1. Bake the unpeeled celeriac in an ovenproof dish until soft, approx. 1½ –2 hours. Cut away the peel and cut the baked celeriac into largish pieces.

2. Slice the celery stalk finely and place in cold water.

3. Cut the figs into wedges.

4. Peel and segment the grapefruit (see page 98).

5. Peel and finely chop the shallot.

6. Make a vinaigrette with the olive oil, red wine vinegar, shallot, salt and black pepper.

7. Divide the celeriac, celery stalk and figs onto 4 plates and drizzle over the vinaigrette.

8. Top with the grapefruit segments, crumbled chèvre and cut cress.

SEGMENTING CITRUS

This is how you get nice segments of citrus fruit:

1. Cut off the top and bottom of the fruit.

2. Peel all around the fruit with a small sharp knife. Make sure to remove all the white pith under the skin.

3. Cut along the membranes around each segment to remove the fillets.

4. Press and save the juice from the remaining fruit. It is the best juice you can lay your hands on.

TARTARE OF BEEF

Tartare in all its forms has been on the menu of almost every restaurant I've worked in. You can make it in so many ways with all kinds of accompaniments and it can sometimes even seem a bit difficult and confusing to the palate. So I have chosen the most simple variant, where the quality of the meat is in focus, while the soy in the mayonnaise is there to elevate the flavours.

My initial thought was to heighten the flavour with a splash of birch sap, which I think has a pleasant sweetness and complements the dish well. Unfortunately, I had to face the fact that the demand for birch sap has declined and consequently it might be difficult to get hold of. If, however, you manage to get your hands on some, I recommend that you add a few drops when you season the meat.

400 g (14 oz) sirloin steak
1 shallot
1 tbs olive oil
1 punnet watercress
salt, black pepper

MAYONNAISE
2 egg yolks
½ tsp dijon mustard
½ tsp white wine vinegar
2 tsp tamari
500 ml (17 fl oz/2 cups) cooking oil or canola (rapeseed) oil
salt

1. Chop the steak finely.
2. Peel and finely chop the shallot and mix into the chopped meat.
3. Add olive oil, salt and pepper.

MAYONNAISE
1. Whisk together the egg yolks, mustard, vinegar and tamari.
2. While whisking, carefully pour in the oil, drop by drop at first and then in a fine drizzle, until all is used.
3. Add salt to taste.

Place the meat on 4 plates and dot the mayonnaise over the tartare. Cut the watercress over the top and finish off with a few turns of the pepper mill. Serve the tartare with some toast.

PORK SCHNITZEL WITH BEANS AND GREEN LEAVES

Pork, veal or chicken – there are many ways to make this dish, which is often neglected when cooking at home. I have eaten this Austrian speciality many, many times in restaurants on the ski slopes in Austria, Switzerland and Germany. And I love to make it myself in all its forms. But my love for this alpine classic was sparked as a young boy in a small, family owned restaurant under the ski lift in Åre, with my father and family. With a Swedish-Austrian chef at the stove, classic wienerschnitzels of the highest quality were prepared.

Little did I know that I myself would be making this dish in a kitchen in the Alps twenty years later.

4 carrots
50 g yellow wax beans
50 g green beans
1 bunch radishes
2 eggs
60 g (2 oz) plain (all-purpose) flour
80 g (2¾ oz) breadcrumbs
4 pork schnitzels
200 g (7 oz) butter
250 g (9 oz) mangold or spinach
2 tbs capers
juice of 1 lemon
salt

1. Peel and cut the carrots on the diagonal. Boil in lightly salted water for 3–4 minutes.

2. Halve the beans and boil in salted water for approx. 1 minute.

3. Quarter the radishes.

4. Whisk the eggs in a bowl. Put the flour and breadcrumbs onto 2 plates.

5. Coat the schnitzels in the flour, then dip them in the egg. Finally, coat them with the breadcrumbs. Season with salt.

6. Fry the schnitzels in the butter over a medium heat until golden brown on both sides. It takes around 3 minutes per side.

7. Remove the schnitzels and stir the mangold and radishes round in the frying butter, add the capers and lemon juice.

Serve the schnitzels with the vegetables and the green leaves.

Note!

If you want to make schnitzels from scratch, then fillet of pork, veal or chicken breast are three good choices. Flatten 4 equal pieces thinly but not so they start to disintegrate. In restaurants we have a special tool for this, but for the home cook a saucepan will do the trick. Just be careful not to damage your worktop!

CARBONARA

Here is a great opportunity to take stock of the range of locally produced cheeses, as many ski resorts are known for their local food products. Maybe your village has its own cheese shop with a fantastic selection of high-quality cheeses? In that case, take the opportunity to visit it because in this simple, easy-to-make and above all, delicious dish, the cheese plays the leading role.

500 g (1 lb 2 oz) penne pasta

150 g (5½ oz) pancetta, cut in small pieces

2 tbs olive oil

2 garlic cloves, finely grated

6 egg yolks

120 g (4½ oz) grated parmesan or similar hard cheese

a good handful thyme

salt, black pepper

1. Boil the pasta according to the instructions on the packet. Reserve roughly 200 ml (7 fl oz) of the cooking water.

2. Fry the pancetta in a frying pan with the olive oil until crispy. Add the garlic towards the end.

3. In a bowl, combine the egg yolks with the parmesan and add 3 tbs of the cooled down pasta water.

4. Mix the pancetta with the pasta and stir in the egg and parmesan mixture.

5. Add more pasta water to achieve a creamy consistency.

6. Add salt and plenty of freshly ground black pepper.

7. Serve the carbonara in a bowl and top with fresh plucked sprigs of thyme.

VEAL MEATBALLS IN A RICH TOMATO SAUCE

It's impressive how the Italians are able to make such fantastically good-tasting food. But good ingredients aren't enough – joy and passion are just as important. To devote a few extra minutes to the finishing touches is more important than many people realise. One Italian classic is meatballs in tomato sauce. The sauce plays the leading role and, to be successful, those extra minutes are essential for its rich, flavourful taste.

TOMATO SAUCE
1 onion
2 garlic cloves
3 tbs olive oil
1 tbs tomato purée
1 tsp dried oregano
1 tbs dried basil
100 ml (3½ fl oz) white wine
100 ml (3½ fl oz) water
½ stock cube (5 g/⅛ oz)
600 g (1 lb 5 oz) crushed
   tomatoes
1 tbs honey
1 tsp salt
½ tsp black pepper

MEATBALLS
1 onion
1 garlic clove
500 g (1 lb 2 oz) minced veal
1 egg
2 tbs water
1 tsp salt
fresh basil or oregano
parmesan

1. Peel and finely chop the onion and garlic. Sauté the onions and garlic in the olive oil until soft, together with the tomato purée, oregano and basil.

2. Add the wine, water and the stock cube. Boil until most of the water evaporates.

3. Pour in the crushed tomatoes, honey, salt and black pepper. Simmer over a low heat for approx. 15 minutes while you prepare the meatballs.

MEATBALLS

1. Grate the onion and garlic and stir them into the minced veal, egg, water and salt.

2. Finely chop and mix in the herbs. Shape the mixture into 18–20 balls.

3. Place the meatballs in the tomato sauce and simmer for 10–15 minutes.

Serve the meatballs with pasta and grated parmesan. Top with more fresh basil or oregano.

BAKED BACK FILLET OF COD WITH SANDEFJORD SAUCE

I learnt how to make this sauce in Norway at my first workplace. It's easy – both to make and remember – the recipe consists of equal parts cream, crème fraîche and butter. Despite this, it is, as always, important to taste the sauce often to achieve the best results. Sandefjord sauce goes with both fish and shellfish – here I serve it with cod.

OVEN: 90°C (195°F)

80 g (2¾ oz) salt

2 litres (68 fl oz/8 cups) water

600 g (1 lb 5 oz) back fillet of cod, skin removed

cooking oil

500 g (1 lb 2 oz) broccoli

1 punnet cress

a handful dill

a handful chives

100 ml (3½ fl oz) cream

100 g (3½ oz) crème fraîche

100 g (3½ oz) butter

juice of 1 lemon

1 tbs olive oil

3 tbs trout roe

salt

1. Dissolve the salt in the water and cure the cod in it for 10 minutes.

2. Pour a few drops of oil into an ovenproof dish. Cut the cod into 4 pieces and place it in the dish. Bake in the oven until the inner temperature of the fish reaches 43–44°C (109–111°F).

3. Cut the broccoli into florets.

4. Shave 4 of the florets into thin slices and place them in cold water to crisp up.

5. Boil the rest of the broccoli in salted water for approx. 3 minutes.

6. Cut the cress, pluck the dill and cut the chives finely.

7. Bring the cream and crème fraîche to the boil. Add the butter, half the lemon juice and some salt.

8. Remove the shaved broccoli from the water and combine with the olive oil.

9. Place a piece of fish on each plate and surround it with boiled broccoli, the shaved broccoli, cress and dill.

10. Fold the chives and trout roe into the sauce and drizzle it over the fish.

ROASTED CAULIFLOWER WITH PORK BELLY AND BEARNAISE SAUCE

Most people probably associate bearnaise sauce with a large piece of meat, but here the vegetable plays the leading role. And I think the sauce works just as well with a vegetable, if not better. Butter and cabbage is a combination I often use in my cooking. Roasted or baked cabbage goes incredibly well with this buttery herb sauce.

OVEN: 180°C (360°F)

2 heads of cauliflower

50 g (1¾ oz) + 450 g (1 lb) butter

150 g (5½ oz) pork belly, diced

1 shallot

a handful fresh tarragon

a handful chervil

1 bunch curly parsley

100 ml (3½ fl oz) red wine vinegar

100 ml (3½ fl oz) water

4 egg yolks

cayenne pepper

a handful flat-leaf (Italian) parsley

salt

1. Place the cauliflowers on a baking sheet and shave over the 50 g (1¾ oz) butter. Roast in the oven until golden brown.

2. Fry the pork belly over a medium heat.

3. Peel and chop the shallot.

4. Pluck and finely chop the leaves of the tarragon, chervil and curly parsley. Save the stalks.

5. Melt the remaining butter and let it cool a little.

6. Boil the red wine vinegar, water, shallot and the stalks from the herbs until half the liquid remains. Strain away the onion and stalks.

7. Add the egg yolks to the liquid and whisk over a low heat until the sauce starts to thicken, then remove the pan from the heat.

8. Slowly add the cooled butter in a thin trickle, whisking constantly.

9. Add the herbs, except the flat-leaf parsley, then add salt and a little cayenne pepper to taste.

10. Cover the cauliflower with the bearnaise sauce and pork belly. Top with the flat-leaf parsley.

Note!
Skip the bacon if you want to make the dish vegetarian.

LAMB SHANK WITH A RICH TOMATO SAUCE AND GREMOLATA

To me, Italian cuisine is not only about its simple and rustic fare. What fascinates me is the sense of companionship around the table at meal times, and I've adopted the tradition of serving food on large serving platters. On my adventures, together with my "second family" of fantastic friends, Sunday dinner has gained a whole new meaning. Here is my take on the Italian classic osso buco, although here I make it with lamb shank.

OVEN: 150°C (300°F)

4 lamb shanks (approx. 100 g/3½ oz per person)
2 tbs plain (all-purpose) flour
oil for frying
2 carrots
½ celeriac
1 onion
2 garlic cloves
50 g (1¾ oz) butter
200 ml (7 oz) chicken stock
200 ml (7 oz) white wine
1 tbs tomato purée
400 g (14 oz) crushed tomatoes
a handful fresh thyme
1 bay leaf
salt, black pepper

GREMOLATA
1 lemon
2 garlic cloves
a handful parsley
100 ml (3½ fl oz) olive oil
salt, black pepper

1. Salt and pepper the lamb shanks and coat with the flour.

2. Fry the lamb shanks in oil for 2–3 minutes on each side in an ovenproof (preferably cast-iron) casserole pot.

3. Peel the carrots, celeriac, onion and garlic. Dice the vegetables and grate the garlic.

4. Fry the onion, garlic and root vegetables in a frying pan until soft, then arrange over the lamb shanks.

5. Add the stock, wine, tomato purée, crushed tomatoes, sprigs of thyme and the bay leaf. Cover and cook in the oven for approx. 3 hours or until the meat starts to fall apart.

GREMOLATA

1. Finely grate the lemon zest and garlic.

2. Finely chop the parsley.

3. Squeeze the lemon juice into a bowl. Add the rest of the ingredients, then add salt and black pepper to taste.

This casserole is usually served with risotto, but roast potatoes also go really well with it. Top the lamb shanks with the gremolata and freshly ground black pepper.

DUCK BREAST WITH CARROTS AND BEANS

Duck breasts are easy to turn into an exclusive meal at home. With simple side dishes like carrots, beans and a tasty sauce, this meal is a perfect way of getting into a weekend mood without having to spend hours in the kitchen.

OVEN: 90°C (195°F)

4 duck breasts
1 garlic clove
1 sprig of thyme
1 tbs butter
salt

CARROT PURÉE

4 carrots
1 tbs butter
1 tbs lemon juice
salt

VEGETABLES

2 carrots
100 g (3½ oz) yellow wax
   beans
50 g (1¾ oz) butter
salt

RED WINE SAUCE

2 shallots
1 garlic clove
1 tsp tomato purée
2 sprigs of thyme
2 tbs olive oil
200 ml (7 oz) red wine
300 ml (10 fl oz) veal stock,
   or 1 stock cube (10g/¼ oz)
   + 300 ml (10 fl oz) water
½ tsp cornflour + 1 tbs water
sherry vinegar
salt, black pepper

1. Score the skin of the duck breasts in a criss-cross pattern without cutting all the way through the skin. Add salt and black pepper.

2. Place the duck breasts, skin side down, in a cold frying pan, then fry over a medium heat until the skin is crispy.

3. Crush the garlic and add the thyme, garlic and butter to the pan. Flip the duck breasts and fry quickly on the other side, approx. 30 seconds.

4. Place the duck breasts, skin side up, in an ovenproof dish and bake in the oven until the inside temperature reaches 57°C (135°F).

5. Let the duck breasts rest for 5–10 minutes.

CARROT PURÉE

1. Peel and cut the carrots into pieces. Boil in salted water until soft, approx. 10–12 minutes.

2. Drain the water and blend the carrots with the butter and lemon juice. Salt to taste.

VEGETABLES

1. Peel and cut the carrots lengthways. Cook in salted water until soft, 6–8 minutes.

2. Trim the beans and boil in salted water for 2 minutes. As soon as they are ready, plunge them into cold water to stop further cooking.

3. To serve: melt the butter and warm the carrots and beans in it.

RED WINE SAUCE

1. Peel and chop the shallots and garlic.

2. Fry the shallots, garlic, tomato purée and thyme sprigs in olive oil over a medium heat until the shallots are golden brown.

3. Add the wine and reduce – let it boil – until half the liquid remains.

4. Add the stock and reduce again over a high heat until half the liquid remains – approx. 5 minutes.

5. Strain the sauce and thicken with cornflour stirred into the water. Bring to the boil again.

6. Add a little sherry vinegar, salt and pepper to taste.

OVEN-ROASTED CHICKEN WITH ANCHOVIES AND HERB BUTTER

Chicken is incredibly delicious and easy to prepare. The variations are infinite, which means I never tire of it. And roasting it whole in the oven is a really easy way to cook it, since the chicken takes care of itself. Time for you to relax.

With anchovies, herbs and lemon you bring out the saltiness and the acidity that enhances the taste and aroma of the chicken.

OVEN: 300°C (570°F)

150 g (5½ oz) butter at room
   temperature

6 finely chopped anchovies
   in oil

2 garlic cloves, grated

2 tbs lemon juice

1 tbs finely chopped thyme

½ tbs finely chopped rosemary

salt

1 whole chicken

1 tbs salt flakes

½ tbs sugar

1 lemon

2 onions

black pepper

1. Mix the butter, anchovies, garlic, lemon juice, thyme and rosemary together to make the herb butter. Add salt to taste.

2. Press in and distribute the herb butter evenly under the skin of the chicken. Spread it over the outside of the chicken, too. Pat on salt flakes, sugar and black pepper.

3. Cut the lemon in half and the onions into wedges. Place the lemon and onions around the chicken in a roasting pan.

4. Put the roasting pan in the oven for approx. 25 minutes, then reduce the heat to 150°C (300°F) and continue cooking for a further 45 minutes. The chicken should have a fine, roasted colour and the thigh should have an inner temperature of 80°C (175°F). Baste with the juices while cooking.

5. Serve the chicken with something that can soak up the tasty juices. My personal favourite is freshly cooked bulgur wheat.

FRIED REINDEER WITH POTATO PURÉE, YELLOW BEETS AND HORSERADISH

In Sweden we are proud of our fantastic reindeer and its meat. It has a lovely mild, gamey flavour that is suited to a range of cooking methods – everything from frying or salt-curing to smoking. Here I serve it fried with a buttery potato purée, yellow beetroot and grated horseradish. Sirloin or venison work well as an alternative to reindeer.

OVEN: 120°C (250°F)

4 yellow beetroot

600 g (1 lb 5 oz) reindeer fillet or sirloin

2 tbs olive oil for frying

2 tbs butter for frying

200 g (7 oz) potatoes

50 g (1¾ oz) butter

100 g (3½ oz) crème fraîche

1 tbs white wine vinegar

1 punnet cress

approx. 40 g (1½ oz) fresh horseradish

salt, black pepper

1. Boil the beets, skin on, until soft, 20–40 minutes depending on size. Rinse them in cold water and rub off the skins. Cut into wedges.

2. Divide the meat into 4 equal pieces. Salt and pepper.

3. Brown the meat on all sides over a high heat in the oil and butter.

4. Finish off the meat in the oven until the inner temperature reaches 50°C (120°F). Let rest for 15 minutes.

5. Peel and boil the potatoes in lightly salted water until soft. Pour off the water and press the potatoes through a sieve.

6. Mix the potatoes with butter and crème fraîche. Blend quickly to a smooth, creamy consistency and add salt to taste.

7. Season the beets with the vinegar, salt and black pepper.

8. Spread the potato purée in the middle of 4 plates and place the meat on top.

9. Arrange the beets and cress around it and grate a generous amount of horseradish over everything.

MUSTARD-CREAMED VEGETABLES WITH SPICY SAUSAGES

When I'm at a loss for what to cook, I often end up making something creamed. With a knob of butter, a little flour and a splash of milk, you can make a creamed dish in no time. Creaming is suitable for most things and fills a hungry stomach after a day on the mountain.

½ head pointed cabbage

2 carrots

½ head cauliflower

2 tbs butter

2 tbs plain (all-purpose) flour

500 ml (17 fl oz/2 cups) milk

2 tbs unsweetened coarse grain mustard

a handful parsley, chopped

1 shallot, finely chopped

1 garlic clove, grated

½ tsp salt

4 spicy sausages, such as salsiccia or merguez

1 tsp olive oil

1 punnet watercress

1. Cut the cabbage, carrots and cauliflower into pieces. In separate pans, boil in salted water until soft.

2. Melt the butter in a saucepan and stir in the flour.

3. Add the milk, a little at a time then bring to the boil over a medium heat and simmer for approx. 3 minutes, whisking continuously.

4. Fold the boiled vegetables into the mixture and add the mustard, parsley, shallot and garlic. Salt to taste.

5. Fry the sausages in the oil and serve with the vegetables. Top with cut watercress.

CABBAGE SALAD WITH MINT, LIME AND GARLIC

This taste explosion takes me back to winters in Engelberg. The salad – which has been with me in numerous permutations – was created when the ski bums were pestering me for kebabs. I was not so inclined to cook fast food, in my opinion this felt like a lot more fun. Here the salad is served with a piece of juicy pork shoulder.

CABBAGE SALAD

1 fennel

½ red cabbage

2 sweet red pointed peppers, or 1 red capsicum (bell pepper)

2 spring onions (scallions)

a handful coriander (cilantro)

a handful mint

juice and zest of 2 limes

2 garlic cloves, grated

3 tbs olive oil

1 tsp sugar

½ tsp salt

PORK SHOULDER

½ tsp paprika

½ tsp ground cumin

½ tsp cayenne pepper

½ tsp salt

4 boneless pork shoulder steaks, approx. 600–700 g (1 lb 5 oz–1 lb 9 oz)

olive oil for frying

CABBAGE SALAD

1. Shred the fennel, red cabbage, red peppers and spring onions and place in a bowl.

2. Chop and mix in the coriander and mint.

3. Mix the lime juice and zest, garlic, oil, sugar and salt for a dressing.

4. Pour the dressing into the cabbage mixture, preferably just before serving to maintain the texture of the vegetables.

PORK SHOULDER

1. Mix the spices into a rub and pat it onto the meat.

2. Fry the meat in the olive oil over a high heat, 3–4 minutes each side.

3. Let the meat rest for 5 minutes, slice and serve with the salad.

CHARCUTERIE WITH CONFIDENCE

Which is the greater luxury – eating high-quality primary produce every day, or going full tilt with luxury produce on special occasions?

IT IS EASY TO miss this humble little building on the outskirts of Undersåker on the road between Östersund and Åre, but you should definitely try not to. It is well worth screeching to a halt because, inside, things are happening.

The building houses Undersåkers Charkuterifabrik which was founded by the local food legend Magnus Nilsson (of restaurant Fäviken Magasinet fame). His goal was to refine primary produce of the highest quality from small local producers. These days, Undersåkers is run by a bunch of guys with Tomas Gustafsson at the helm. When I enter the shop, I'm struck by how they have chosen to present their products.

Almost reverentially. The way in which they present the meat is almost museum-like and conveys the fact that it is carefully selected and of the highest quality. Through a window in the premises, you can glimpse the hanging room, where newly smoked sausages hang in neat rows. Good taste and great self-confidence through and through. Transparency throughout the whole chain of production is the motto, something that, to be honest, is a rarity in the preparation of charcuterie, but there is nothing to hide here. Additives are almost non-existent and are used only when they serve to heighten the experience of the product. The vision becomes apparent

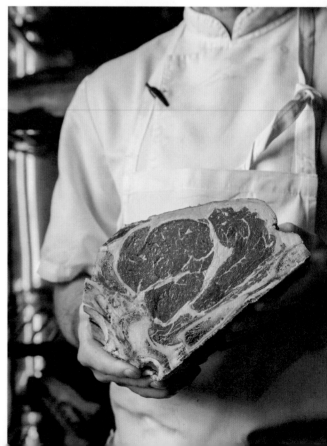

when Tomas says: "What we produce is not meant to be luxury products for the few but everyday food for the many, although it's a lot better than what most of us usually buy, of course."

The challenge is that people in general have a low tolerance to the price of everyday items. This is a constant dilemma for small scale, ambitious producers who have to fight the big shots who have completely different resources and the endurance to claw back from the swings what they lose on the roundabouts.

Undersåkers refine the primary produce: from Falu sausage, black pudding, dried isterband sausage and various smoked sausages, to dazzling aged beef. It is a small-scale and appealing way to work for both the farmers and those who refine their products. In this way, an overview of the whole production chain is maintained with a respect and care for each other that I am convinced benefits the primary produce – and in the end, the consumers.

These meetings with uncompromising, driving spirits makes their dedication to quality over quantity seem obvious. And it's so much simpler to cook good food when you have great ingredients. You don't have to complicate things.

A FEW DAYS LATER we pass Undersåkers again. Today, the carpark is packed. Another screech to a halt. There's a pop-up sausage stand, which means that Tomas is peddling elk sausage topped with a mound of sauerkraut, in hot dog buns baked by Maja in Undersåker, to a steady stream of hungry regulars and a motley crew of others – like Patrik, the photographer, and me.

Tomas's words about great everyday food for the masses pops into my mind again. I take the opportunity to buy a load of goodies to share at home: smoked elk heart, air-dried isterband sausages, Falu sausages, some brawn, pâtés and more. I finish off the brawn and the hot dog in the car on the way back to Stockholm! ❄

CHOOSE MEAT LIKE A CHEF!

There are a few simple things to bear in mind when choosing meat:

• Choose the appropriate cooking method for the cut of meat. Some cuts, such as fillet, require only frying or grilling while others, like shank, need longer cooking and are usually boiled or simmered to become tender. The differences are usually down to the structure of the meat with layers of muscle, fibre and connective tissue.

• Look for meat with fat marbling – that's where the flavour is and it makes a big difference, especially with beef.

• Discuss meat with your butcher or at the meat counter – create a relationship.

• Eat less but better-quality meat.

• Be adventurous, try unusual cuts – not just fillet.

MUSHROOM RISOTTO

This creamy mushroom risotto is easily adaptable depending on what mushrooms, cheese and stock you use. I cook mine with a selection of mixed mushrooms and use mushroom or chicken stock for a richer taste. Find your own favourites!

400 g (14 oz) various mushrooms

100 g (3½ oz) butter

2 shallots

2 garlic cloves

350 g (12½ oz) risotto rice

200 ml (7 fl oz) dry white wine

700 ml (23½ fl oz) warm mushroom or chicken stock (or 2 stock cubes [20g/¾ oz] + 700 ml/ 23½ fl oz water)

80 g (2¾ oz) grated parmesan or other mature hard cheese

salt

a handful flat-leaf (Italian) parsley

1. Trim and fry the mushrooms in some of the butter over a medium heat until nicely coloured, about 4–5 minutes. Add salt and put to the side. Mushrooms really take up salt, so it's important to taste and taste again, right from the start.

2. Peel and finely chop the shallots and garlic. In a saucepan, melt the remaining butter and fry the shallots, garlic and rice.

3. Pour in the wine and let it boil into the rice until absorbed.

4. While stirring, top up the rice with stock, a little at a time, until it is absorbed by the rice. This should take 18–22 minutes altogether. The rice should maintain a slightly harder centre and be firm to the bite.

5. Remove the saucepan from the heat and fold in the cheese and, if necessary, the last of the stock. Add salt to taste.

6. Scoop the rice onto 4 plates and top with the fried mushrooms and chopped parsley.

TORTIGLIONI WITH TOMATOES, CHILLI, CAPERS AND GREEN OLIVES

Here is a real everyday life saver! Quick to make, simple and with few ingredients – pasta, a few vegetables and a piece of mature cheese and this dish is conjured up in just a few minutes.

1 onion
1 garlic clove
1 red chilli
4 tbs olive oil
6 tomatoes
3 tbs capers
150 g (5½ oz) green olives
1 lemon, juice and grated zest
1 tsp salt
400 g (14 oz) tortiglioni
a handful flat-leaf (Italian) parsley
parmesan or other mature hard cheese, to taste
black pepper

1. Peel and finely chop the onion, garlic and chilli. Fry until soft in half of the oil without it taking on colour.

2. Cut the tomatoes into pieces and let them fry along with the onion mixture for a further few minutes.

3. Add the remaining oil and the capers.

4. Slice the olives and add, together with the lemon juice and zest.

5. Add salt and pepper to taste.

6. Boil the pasta according to the instructions on the packet.

7. Top a generous serving of pasta with a couple of substantial ladlefuls of the vegetable ragu and some shredded parsley.

Serve with parmesan on the table for those who want some more. Grated parmesan always elevates a good pasta dish.

BEEF STROGANOFF

I always try to find a personal connection to the food I cook and eat. In the case of beef stroganoff that's hard – perhaps it's time for me to visit the Russian mountains for some unforgettable skiing. I've got my sights set on Krasnaja Poljana and Elbrus, both of them high in the Caucasus mountains. Did you know that Elbrus is the highest mountain in Europe at 5642 metres (18510 feet) above sea level?

500 g (1 lb 2 oz) extra-trimmed rump or sirloin

3 tbs cooking oil

2 onions

50 g (1¾ oz) butter

1 tsp salt

100 ml (3½ fl oz) tomato purée

2 tsp dijon mustard

500 ml (17 fl oz/2 cups) double (thick) cream

½ tsp dried basil

400 g (14 oz) farfalle

juice of ½ lemon

black pepper

a handful basil

1. Cut the meat into 1 cm (½ in) thick strips. Brown in batches in a frying pan over a high heat. Put to one side.

2. Peel and finely chop the onions and fry in butter until soft and lightly browned.

3. Put the meat back into the pan, then add salt and pepper.

4. Add the tomato purée, mustard, cream and basil. Stir well.

5. Let the casserole simmer for 10 minutes.

6. Cook the pasta according to the instructions on the packet.

7. Before serving, add lemon juice and black pepper to the casserole to taste. Serve with the cooked pasta and top with shredded fresh basil.

STEAK WITH SPICED BUTTER AND VINEGAR-BOILED ONIONS

With just one knob of spiced butter, you can easily flavour most things. It's not only ridiculously tasty, it's also very quick to make and excellent for freezing if you want to make a bigger batch. The butter works with meat, fish and vegetables – here it is served with a steak, freshly boiled broccoli and vinegar-boiled onions. It doesn't have to be more complicated than that.

4 short loin beef steaks

2 sprigs of thyme

2 garlic cloves, crushed

100 g (3½ oz) butter

2 shallots

1 tbs olive oil

100 ml (3½ fl oz) red wine vinegar

½ tsp sugar

500 g (1 lb 2 oz) broccoli

salt, black pepper

flaked salt

SPICED BUTTER

400 g (14 oz) butter at room temperature

1 garlic clove, grated

2 tsp dijon mustard

1 tsp sambal oelek

1 tsp brandy

1 tbs tomato purée

1 tsp worcestershire sauce

1 pinch cayenne pepper

1 pinch curry powder

1 tsp salt

a handful chervil, chopped

a handful parsley, chopped

a handful chives, chopped

1. Salt and pepper the meat and fry with the thyme and garlic in butter over a high heat, 2–3 minutes per side. I like my meat medium, with an inner temperature of 55°C (130°F) when rested.

2. Peel and finely chop the shallots and fry in the oil over a medium heat without them taking on colour. Add the vinegar and sugar and let the shallots soften.

3. Divide the broccoli into large florets and boil in lightly salted water for approx. 3 minutes.

4. When serving, combine the broccoli and vinegared onions and top with the flaked salt.

SPICED BUTTER

1. Mix all the ingredients carefully for the spiced butter. Mix to ensure that the spices are evenly distributed.

2. Put into a bowl and enjoy with the steak and the freshly boiled broccoli.

FISH STEW WITH TOMATO, CHILLI, SAFFRON AND ORANGE

The variations and interpretations of this fish stew from the south of France are too numerous to count, but I know how I like it! With a hint of heat from the chillies contrasting with the mild flavour of saffron and the freshness of the orange, I think I have found my interpretation. Even the cooking of the fish makes a difference and I choose to cook it separately for best results.

**OVEN: CROUTONS 175°C (345°F),
FISH 100°C (210°F)**

---

2 carrots
1 fennel
1 celery stalk
1 onion
1 garlic clove
1 red chilli
3 tbs olive oil
2 tbs tomato purée
400 g (14 oz) crushed tomatoes
200 ml (7 fl oz) dry white wine
800 ml (27 fl oz) fish or
   shellfish stock
½ g saffron
½ orange, grated zest
1 bay leaf
200 g (7 oz) salmon
200 g (7 oz) cod
olive oil
salt
chives, dill for garnishing

CROUTONS
2 slices of sourdough bread
3 tbs olive oil

AIOLI
200 ml (7 fl oz) mayonnaise
1 garlic clove, finely grated
juice of ½ lemon
salt

1. Cut the carrots, fennel, celery and onion into pieces. Chop the garlic and chilli. Fry the vegetables and chilli in oil.

2. Add the tomato purée and fry for another minute.

3. Add the crushed tomatoes, wine, stock, saffron, orange zest and bay leaf.

4. Let simmer for 15–20 minutes and add salt to taste.

5. Cut the fish into even pieces, 2 × 2 cm (¾ × ¾ in). Add a little salt. Place on a lightly oiled oven sheet.

6. When the stew, croutons and aioli are ready it's time to put the fish in the oven, cook for approx. 7–9 minutes.

7. Place the fish and the croutons on top of the stew and garnish with finely cut chives and dill.

8. Top with a generous spoonful of aioli.

CROUTONS

1. Cut the bread into cubes, approx 1 × 1 cm (½ × ½ in) and drizzle the oil over them.

2. Toast in the oven until crispy and golden brown.

AIOLI

1. Mix the mayonnaise, garlic and lemon juice together. Add salt to taste.

COQ AU VIN

Around the dining table in Chamonix in France, not only memories and stories were created, but also great meals. We all had a great interest in food and wine and made sure to always serve French delicacies for starters while the casserole dishes were simmering away on their own. Coq au vin was an obvious choice – a rich casserole with chicken, smoked pork belly and wine.

100 g (3½ oz) smoked pork belly
2 onions
1 garlic clove
2 carrots
1.2 kg (2 lb 10 oz) chicken thighs
cooking oil
a handful thyme
1 tsp tomato purée
400 ml (13½ fl oz) chicken stock
400 ml (13½ fl oz) red wine
2 bay leaves
6 button mushrooms
1 tsp cornflour + 1 tbs water
a handful flat-leaf (Italian) parsley
salt, black pepper

1. Cut the pork belly into cubes.

2. Peel and chop the onions and garlic. Peel the carrots and cut into large pieces.

3. Salt and pepper the chicken thighs and brown them in oil over a medium heat. Place in a large casserole dish.

4. Fry the pork belly until crispy and put to the side. Chop the thyme.

5. Fry the vegetables lightly and add tomato purée towards the end. Put them into the casserole dish together with the chicken stock, wine, thyme, bay leaves and the fried pork.

6. Bring to the boil and cook, covered, for 25–30 minutes.

7. Cut the button mushrooms into pieces and fry them in a little oil. Add to the casserole and simmer for a further 10 minutes.

8. Mix the cornflour and water and add to thicken the casserole.

9. Chop the parsley and sprinkle over when serving.

There is an obvious choice for a side dish: potato purée!

BAKED CHAR WITH CABBAGE AND WHITE WINE SAUCE

I have never had an interest in fishing, despite living close to the water for most of my life. But I was always the first in line to meet the local fisherman on Friday mornings to select my favourite kinds of fish. The fish was later served to me at the family dining table. I think it was there my interest in cooking fish perfectly was born.

OVEN: 90°C (195°F)

1 tsp salt
4 char fillets
1 tbs olive oil
2 shallots
400–500 g (14 oz–1 lb 2 oz) Savoy cabbage
100 g (3½ oz) butter
2 tbs trout roe
a handful dill
salt

WHITE WINE SAUCE
1 shallot
1 garlic clove
½ fennel
1 + 1 tbs butter
300 ml (10 fl oz) white wine
300 ml (10 fl oz) fish stock or ½ fish stock cube (5 g/⅛ oz) + 200 ml (7 fl oz) water
100 ml (3½ fl oz) milk
300 ml (10 fl oz) cream

1. Salt and rub the char fillets with the olive oil. Place them on a baking sheet with the skin side up.

2. Cook in the oven until the inner temperature reaches 44°C (110°F).

3. Pull off the skin before serving.

4. Peel and slice the shallots thinly.

5. Cut the Savoy cabbage into strips, approx. 4 cm (1½ in) wide.

6. Fry the shallots and cabbage until soft without taking on colour. Add salt to taste.

7. Top the char with the onion and cabbage mixture, trout roe and plucked dill. Top with a generous amount of sauce.

WHITE WINE SAUCE

1. Peel and slice the shallot, garlic and fennel.

2. Melt 1 tbs butter in a saucepan and fry the vegetables for 3 minutes, without taking on colour.

3. Add the wine, bring to the boil and reduce until half of the liquid remains.

4. Add the stock and reduce until 200 ml (7 fl oz) remains.

5. Pour in the milk and cream and reduce further for 4–6 minutes. Strain the sauce and pour back into the saucepan. Mix in 1 tbs butter when serving.

PAN-SEARED SALMON WITH CAULIFLOWER AND HERB MISO

During three of my seasons in the Alps, every Tuesday night ended with a music quiz set by my colleague and friend Jonas. We had a dish of the day on the menu and on Tuesdays it was always salmon. A crowd of regulars from the village would come over for the quiz and to eat the dish of the day, and thus the renowned "Tuesday salmon" was created. It wasn't as if I denied them the rest of the menu – they made their own decision to try to find their favourite salmon of the season. The winner was pan-seared salmon with cauliflower and herb miso, where the miso plays the leading role with its richness, saltiness and umami.

OVEN: 140°C (285°F)

200 g (7 oz) cherry tomatoes

2 tbs miso

1 red chilli

1 garlic clove, grated

a handful flat-leaf (Italian) parsley

a handful tarragon

100 ml (3½ fl oz) cooking oil

2 tbs lemon juice

1 cauliflower

1 bunch kale

600 g (1 lb 5 oz) salmon, skin on

salt

1. Halve the tomatoes and spread them on a baking sheet covered with baking paper. Salt lightly and dry them in the oven for 1 hour.

2. Blend the miso, half of the chilli, garlic, parsley, tarragon and oil with a stick blender.

3. Add lemon juice to taste and possibly a little salt.

4. Cut the cauliflower into florets and boil in salted water until soft, approx. 3 minutes.

5. Cut the stems off the kale and tear the leaves into pieces. Boil quickly in lightly salted water, approx. 2 minutes.

6. Cut the salmon into 4 even pieces and salt lightly.

7. Heat a frying pan, preferably cast-iron, over a high heat. When the pan is smoking, add the salmon pieces and sear them for 1 minute on each side, starting with the skin side down. When salmon is cooked over a high heat, the inner temperature continues to rise after it has been seared – hence the short time in the pan.

8. Chop the rest of the chilli. Mix the tomatoes, cauliflower and kale into a salad, top with the chilli and add a little herb miso to taste.

9. Put the vegetables and salmon on 4 plates with a generous spoonful of herb miso. Pair with a good white wine and enjoy.

PORCHETTA WITH FENNEL AND CARROT SALAD

Yet again, a favourite from the Italian cuisine. With a rich taste of sage, rosemary and fennel, this pork dish is perfect for an evening meal. I hope you'll be as delighted as I am!

OVEN: 140°C (285°F)
—

1 kg (2 lb 3 oz) porchetta,
   or 1 kg (2 lb 3 oz) pork belly
   with rind
a good handful rosemary
a good handful sage
1 tsp fennel seeds
2 garlic cloves
2 tbs olive oil
100 ml (3½ fl oz) water
salt, black pepper

SALAD
3 carrots
1 fennel
2 apples
55 g (2 oz) roasted hazelnuts,
   with skins
juice and zest of 1 lemon
2 tbs olive oil
1 punnet cress
salt

1. Cut the meat lengthways, almost all the way through, so you can fold it out like a book.

2. Finely chop the rosemary, sage, fennel seeds and garlic and mix them together.

3. Salt and pepper the meat and rub the meat with the herb mixture.

4. Roll the meat in the same direction it was folded out from: start from the long side that has no rind and roll so that the rind ends up on the outside. Tie the roll together with kitchen string.

5. Put the meat in an ovenproof dish and drizzle over the olive oil and water.

6. Roast the meat in the oven to an inner temperature of 90°C (195°F), about 3–4 hours. Take out the meat.

7. Increase the oven temperature to 250°C (480°F) and put the meat in again. Roast until the rind starts to get crispy, 7–10 minutes.

SALAD

1. Peel and thinly slice the carrots and the fennel with a potato peeler or mandolin. Put in cold water in the fridge for approx. 20 minutes.

2. Rinse the apples carefully and cut into long narrow pieces.

3. Chop the hazelnuts coarsely.

4. Pour off the water and combine the carrots, fennel, apples and hazelnuts in a bowl.

5. Add lemon juice and zest, olive oil and salt to taste.

6. Top the salad with the cress.

Cut the porchetta into slices approx. 1 cm (½ in) thick and serve with the salad.

RAW-FRIED PUMPKIN WITH PARMESAN AND TRUFFLES

Here is a simplified version of a side dish that was on the plate when my good friend Adam and I had the opportunity to represent Sweden in an international cookery championship: the final of the Bocuse d'Or in 2013. We stood in the test kitchen for six months and created different variations of side dishes for the obligatory main course: fillet of beef. We finally decided on pumpkin and broccoli in combination with parmesan and almonds. Over the years, the dish has developed with the addition of another component, fresh truffles – a simple way of making the everyday luxurious.

1 butternut pumpkin
50 g (1¾ oz) butter
500 g (1 lb 2 oz) broccoli
60 g (2 oz) blanched, roasted almonds
20 g (¾ oz) fresh truffles
40 g (1½ oz) parmesan or other mature hard cheese

1. Peel the pumpkin and slice it lengthways. Remove the seeds with a spoon and cut the pumpkin into pieces, approx. 3 × 3 cm (1¼ × 1¼ in).

2. Fry the pumpkin in the butter over a medium heat until golden and soft all the way through.

3. Divide the broccoli into florets and boil in lightly salted water for 2–3 minutes.

4. Chop the almonds coarsely.

5. Layer the pumpkin and broccoli on 4 plates and top with the grated parmesan, grated truffles and almonds.

Note!
Don't forget to save the butter from the pumpkin frying. It gives dishes a pleasant sweetness you won't want to miss.

HOT CHICKEN WITH A SALAD OF BEAN SPROUTS, BROCCOLI AND A SOY DIP

This dish has been around for a long time during my years as a chef. It's quick to make and you can make it completely vegetarian. I usually use chicken, but marinated tofu is a great alternative for those who want a greener meal.

600 g (1 lb 5 oz) boneless chicken thighs, without skin

3 eggs

60 g (2 oz) plain (all-purpose) flour

70 g (2½ oz) Panko or breadcrumbs

3 tbs sriracha (hot chilli sauce)

6 tbs ketchup (tomato sauce)

2 tbs honey

1 tbs tamari

juice and finely grated zest of 2 limes

½ tsp salt

1 litre (34 fl oz/4 cups) frying oil

MARINATED TOFU

1 tbs grated ginger

1 finely chopped red chilli

1 garlic clove, grated

100 ml (3½ fl oz) tamari

1 tbs sesame oil

400 g (14 oz) tofu

FOR CRUMBING

60 g (2 oz) plain (all-purpose) flour

3 eggs

70 g (2½ oz) Panko or breadcrumbs

SOY DIP

200 ml (7 fl oz) mayonnaise

1 tbs tamari

½ tsp sesame oil

salt

SALAD

500 g (1 lb 5 oz) broccoli

2 carrots

4 spring onions (scallions)

1 garlic clove, finely grated

100 ml (3½ fl oz) cooking oil

a handful of coriander

1 bunch chives

200 g (7 oz) bean sprouts

juice and grated zest of 2 limes

salt

CHICKEN

1. Halve the chicken thighs down the middle.

2. Whisk the eggs.

3. Coat the chicken in flour, dip in the egg batter and cover in Panko.

4. Mix the sriracha, ketchup, honey, tamari and lime to make a chilli dressing. Add salt to taste.

5. Heat the frying oil in a saucepan to 180°C (360°F) and fry the chicken pieces for 3–4 minutes.

6. Remove the chicken pieces, salt them and lay them down in the chilli dressing.

7. Serve immediately – the chicken is at its best when freshly cooked.

Note!

Monitor the temperature of the oil. It easily drops quickly while frying. Another tip is to always fry in a saucepan where the oil only takes up a third of the pan's volume. This stops the oil from boiling over.

MARINATED TOFU

1. Whisk together the ginger, chilli, garlic, tamari and sesame oil.

2. Cut the tofu into cubes approx. 2 × 2 cm (¾ x ¾ in) and put them into the marinade.

3. Leave for at least 1 hour.

4. Coat the tofu in the same way as the chicken with flour, eggs and Panko –and fry.

5. Turn them in the chilli dressing after frying in the same way as the chicken.

SOY DIP

Mix the mayonnaise, tamari and sesame oil. Add salt to taste.

SALAD

1. Cut the broccoli into florets and boil in lightly salted water, approx. 2 minutes.

2. Slice the carrots and spring onions thinly.

3. Mix the garlic and oil and leave for 15 minutes.

4. Shred the coriander and chives.

5. Combine the broccoli, carrots, spring onions, sprouts and coriander.

6. Add the garlic, oil mix, lime and salt to taste. Top with the chives.

SAFFRON RISOTTO WITH BLUE MUSSELS

I was only three years old when I ordered my first classic meal at a restaurant: moules marinière. At that time, the mussels were served with the usual accompaniment, fries. In this recipe, I use a completely different side dish: a risotto. The flavour of saffron, the golden yellow colour and the aroma make a seductive combination with the freshly cooked mussels.

2 kg (4 lb 6 oz) blue mussels
1 shallot
1 garlic clove
½ head fennel
2 tbs olive oil
300 ml (10 fl oz) dry white wine
600 ml (20½ fl oz) water

RISOTTO
1 shallot
1 garlic clove
50 ml (1¾ fl oz) olive oil
300 g (10½ oz) risotto rice
700–800 ml (23½–27 fl oz) mussel stock
1 pinch saffron
50 g (1¾ oz) butter
80 g (2¾ oz) grated parmesan
salt

MUSSELS

1. Rinse the mussels under running water. Pull away any beard (the little hairy tuft that often sticks out from the shell).

2. Gently tap the mussels on the worktop if they are open. Discard any mussels that do not shut and those that are broken.

3. Peel and finely chop the shallot, garlic and fennel. Fry them in oil in a large saucepan for approx. 3 minutes, without taking on colour.

4. Pour in the wine and water. Boil for 2 minutes, covered.

5. Add the mussels and boil vigorously for 3–5 minutes, covered, until the mussels open.

6. Remove the mussels, strain the liquid and save it for the risotto.

RISOTTO

1. Peel and chop the shallot and garlic finely. Carefully fry in the olive oil in a frying pan over a medium heat.

2. Pour in the rice and continue frying for approx. 2 minutes without it taking on colour.

3. Pour in the stock, a little at a time, allowing it to absorb fully into the rice before adding more. Use 2 tbs of the mussel stock to mix with the saffron. Add the saffron mix after approx. half the cooking time.

4. When the rice is perfectly boiled, 17–20 minutes – soft but with a small, firmer centre – stir in the butter.

5. Put the pan to the side and add the parmesan.

6. Add salt to taste.

Serve the risotto immediately, together with the mussels and gremolata (see page 114).

KALE AND WALNUT PESTO

Cabbage is one of my absolute favourite vegetables. I love all kinds of brassicas. I even flavour my pesto with kale, which does not only make it delicious but also adds lots of vitamins.

100 g (3½ oz) fresh kale, stalks removed

½ tsp salt

80 g (2¾ oz) roasted walnuts

1 garlic clove

a good handful basil

40 g (1½ oz) grated parmesan or other mature hard cheese

200 ml (7 fl oz) olive oil

1 tbs lemon juice

salt, black pepper

1 packet spaghetti

1. Shred the kale and boil until soft in plenty of lightly salted water, approx. 3 minutes.

2. Strain the kale in a colander and immediately rinse with cold water to stop further cooking. Squeeze out the last bit of liquid with your hand.

3. Blend the walnuts coarsely for approx. 15 seconds, using a stick blender.

4. Grate the garlic finely.

5. Blend the kale, basil, garlic and grated cheese. Mix in the walnuts.

6. Add the oil, then salt, lemon juice and black pepper to taste.

Serve the pesto with spaghetti. If you, against all odds, have any pesto left over, it can be kept in the fridge for a couple of days without losing flavour.

PORK LOIN WITH SWEDE PURÉE AND BEANS

An oven-roasted pork loin always tastes excellent and if you serve it with a buttery swede (rutabaga) purée and a spicy bean salad you will make your friends and family very happy.

OVEN: 90°C (195°F)

PORK LOIN
600 g (1 lb 5 oz) piece of boneless pork loin

a handful thyme

2 tbs olive oil

2 tbs butter

2 garlic cloves, whole

salt, black pepper

SWEDE PURÉE
600 g (1 lb 5 oz) peeled swede (rutabaga)

50 g (1¾ oz) butter

½ tsp salt

a handful tarragon

BEANS
200 g (7 oz) green beans

1 shallot

2 tbs grainy mustard (preferably made with cider vinegar)

2 tbs olive oil

juice of ½ lemon

salt, black pepper

PORK LOIN

1. Rub the meat with the salt, pepper and chopped thyme.

2. Brown in oil on all sides. Add the butter and garlic and baste the meat for about 1 minute while frying.

3. Place the loin in an ovenproof dish and roast in the oven until the inner temperature reaches 59°C (138°F). Let the meat rest for 15 minutes before carving.

SWEDE PURÉE

1. Cut the swede into equal pieces and boil in lightly salted water until soft.

2. Blend the swede with the butter until smooth. Add salt to taste.

3. Top the swede purée with tarragon.

BEANS

1. Trim and boil the beans in lightly salted water for 2 minutes. Slice the shallot thinly.

2. Mix the beans, shallot, mustard, oil and lemon juice together. Add salt and pepper to taste.

Place a bed of bean salad on every plate and put the meat on top. Serve the swede purée on the side.

PORK CHOPS WITH SPICY CORN AND BROCCOLI

One of my favourite accompaniments to a nice piece of meat is lightly creamed spicy corn. It provides both heat and acidity, which is balanced by the cream. Together with a juicy and well-fried pork chop, this is a dish that's hard to beat. Try it with a light, cold beer.

4 pork chops
2 tbs cooking oil
2 tbs butter
salt
1 tin of sweetcorn (400g/14 oz)
1 garlic clove, grated
1 tbs butter
1 pinch chilli flakes
300 ml (10 fl oz) whipping cream
250 g (9 oz) broccoli
a good handful coriander (cilantro)
a handful chives
1 red chilli
2 limes
salt, black pepper

1. Salt and fry the chops in the oil over a high heat for approx. 2 minutes on each side. Add the butter and continue frying for a minute or so.

2. Remove the chops and let them rest for about 10 minutes.

3. Strain the liquid from the sweetcorn.

4. Fry the garlic in butter over a low heat. Add the chilli flakes.

5. Add the cream and sweetcorn and simmer over a low heat for approx. 10 minutes.

6. Slice the broccoli into even florets and boil until soft in lightly salted water, approx. 2 minutes.

7. Fold the broccoli into the corn mixture. Add salt and pepper to taste.

8. Finely shred the coriander, chives and chilli. Fold the coriander into the corn mixture and top with the chives and chilli.

9. Cut the limes in half and press the juice over the mixture and the chops at the table.

LEG OF LAMB WITH WARM TOMATO AND BEAN SALAD

When I was a child, the family would often gather for a relaxed Sunday dinner to round up the week. Keep this tradition alive and invite your friends for a tasty Sunday roast with simple accompaniments. Sunday dinner has been a standing tradition, even during my years in Switzerland, and has resulted in friends and memories for life.

OVEN: 120°C (250°F)

800 g (1 lb 12 oz) boneless leg of lamb, preferably tied

2 tbs butter

2 garlic cloves

a handful sage

TOMATO AND BEAN SALAD

2 garlic cloves

1 onion

4 tbs olive oil

400 g (14 oz) cooked white beans

6 tomatoes

juice and zest of ½ lemon

a handful flat-leaf (Italian) parsley

salt, black pepper

1. In a frying pan, brown the lamb in butter on all sides until golden brown.

2. Add 2 crushed garlic cloves and the sage sprigs, and fry for about a minute more. Take out the meat and place it on an oven rack.

3. Roast in the oven to an inner temperature of 56°C (133°F).

4. Remove the roast and let it rest while you prepare the rest of the meal.

TOMATO AND BEAN SALAD

1. Finely chop 2 garlic cloves and the onion. Fry in olive oil until soft without taking on colour.

2. Rinse the beans and stir them into the onion.

3. Cut the tomatoes into pieces, approx. 1 cm (½ in), add to the beans and onion and fry for a further 2–3 minutes.

4. Add the lemon juice, lemon zest, salt and a generous amount of black pepper to taste.

5. Stir in the chopped parsley when serving.

Roast potatoes work a treat as a side dish.

RAGU AND RANDONNÉE

"It's all about the farm", reads a sign on the fridge. But the skis and snowshoes leaning against the wood pile outside the house, still dripping with snow, tell me that for the former French ski mountaineering champion Léonie Ferran, it's just as much about the mountains.

MERCANTOUR IS a large and wild national park in the Alpes-Maritimes in south-eastern France. It's not exactly the first area I think about when I dream of skiing on high mountains! But the fact is that this southern part of the Alps, which stretches all the way down to the turquoise waters of the Mediterranean is – for most people – an undiscovered pearl. And I had heard from many sources about Gîte Ferran, a little guest house and farm deep within this national park. Lured by the rumours of good locally produced food, fantastic skiing and great hospitality, I figured it was a place I had to visit.

THE PHOTOGRAPHER, PATRIK, AND I start our journey in the countryside surrounding Nice and drive north in the Tinée valley. The road that follows the River Var upstream in the mountains soon turns spectacular. It undulates through deep ravines and, every now and then, I glimpse a small mountain village perched like an eagle's nest on a plateau high on the mountain. The last stretch up to the small village of Estenc, situated 1800 m (5905 ft) above sea level, runs through a small and deep ravine that leaves me completely breathless. Here, the cliff walls are first brick red, a colour that, a few kilometres later, shifts and turns black as coal. Mercantour has been a protected nature reserve for more than 20 years and contains a rich fauna that includes mountain goats, deer, golden eagles and wolves, even though we are only 110 kilometres (68 miles) from the coast.

Situated by the source of the River Var, the village has 17 inhabitants, seven of which belong to the Ferran family. The final stretch down to the farm itself is just a small gravel road. We pass a barn and a bit further on, at the end of the road, lies the small farm with a breathtaking view down towards the valley. The first thing that strikes us as we exit the car is the silence, only broken by the distant cackling of the farm's chickens. We have arrived in paradise!

"Perhaps we have a battle on our hands: tonight she's cooking dinner for me, the competitive star chef, and I'm invited on a randonnée, a hike, up the mountain tomorrow."

A CERTAIN ANXIETY HAS, however, been mounting during our car journey: what if our somewhat fractured French email conversation has not only been a cause for laughter but also led to misunderstandings. Maybe they haven't realised that we were arriving today?

We could not have been more wrong. When we find Léonie, she is in the middle of preparing everything for the arrival of today's guests. She receives us with a big smile and open arms. She immediately stops everything she is doing and enthusiastically starts to show us around the farm. She talks lovingly of all the animals they have and shows us the beautiful rooms where we will be sleeping. She speaks energetically about future plans for her guest house and her farm.

Last but not least, we are welcomed into the holy of holies: the kitchen. It is lovely and of a high and modern standard and, despite a certain reticence, I note Léonie's pride in what is the heart of her little enterprise. This is where she will conjure up a four-course menu for us in just a few hours' time. She is curious about my background as a chef and I sense her quiet approval when I tell her about my working life, that I also like to compete in culinary competitions and that I coach the Swedish Junior Chefs National Team.

The conversation gradually shifts to our next mutual passion: skiing. Léonie tells me that she was born and bred on the farm and that, from the age of 11, she skied with her brothers over the mountain pass to school in the larger neighbouring village of Barcelonnette. Her brothers – not surprisingly – work as mountain guides and she mentions in passing that, in 2007, at just 17, she became the French ski mountaineering champion and was, for many years, part of the French national team. I am obviously impressed but at the same time I wonder whether perhaps we have a battle on our hands: tonight she's cooking dinner for me, the competitive star chef, and I'm invited on a randonnée, a hike, up the mountain tomorrow.

We are both competitive people.

IT IS STILL early in the afternoon and we are many hours away from dinner, so Léonie suggests that Patrik and I get some skiing in before the meal, while she carries on with her activities on the farm and in the guest house. In a few short sentences she explains that we can put on our skis behind the barn and keep going up to the left until we reach a plateau. Her attitude to the mountains and skiing sounds very uncomplicated and obvious.

The sun is persistent and it is at least 15°C (59°F), despite the fact that it is only the end of

"With the sun in our faces, we have a great run in the spring snow, with the terrain steepening quite pleasingly here and there."

February. Soon we find our pace and take only short pauses now and then to take off yet another piece of clothing or to put on yet another layer of sunscreen.

We are alone on the mountain and the feeling of being at one with nature is overwhelming.

After a few hours we decide to take off the climbing skins and click in our heels. With the sun in our faces, we have a great run in the spring snow, with the terrain steepening quite pleasingly here and there. The lactic acid kicks in before we are back where we started.

BACK DOWN AGAIN we contentedly lean our skis against the wall of the newly constructed barn. In addition to the sounds of cows mooing, other noises of activity from inside can be heard. Peering in curiously, I am met by Jean, Léonie's husband. He is as warm and welcoming as his wife and speaks animatedly about the cows: the different breeds, how old they are and even their names.

Come evening, we feel the delightful tiredness and hunger you experience after a day up in the mountains with sun and skiing. Gorgeous aromas waft from the kitchen. It's time for what we came here for as much as for the skiing: the food. Léonie's mother, Gudrun, carries one delicious dish after the other into the warm, cosy dining room. First, we are served a pea soup flavoured with orange. Gudrun tells us they have just received the freshly picked oranges from a friend on the coast. Winter is the high season for citrus on the Mediterranean coast. This combination of flavours, new to me, turns out to be absolutely delightful and I memorise it for the future.

The main course is a ragu of rabbit from the farm, served with a creamy potato gratin. For us Scandinavians, rabbit is not usually something that appears on the menu, but here it's more common. I would liken the taste to chicken, but slightly more flavourful, which gives a rich ragu, and I cannot stop myself from having seconds. Gratin Dauphinois, as it is called in French, is a gorgeously creamy potato gratin with lots of garlic that also originates in the mountains. A perfect main course for hungry skiers.

When we think we simply cannot eat any more it is, as always in France, time for cheese – a heavenly home-made goat's cheese with a mild consistency that melts in the mouth.

For dessert, Léonie has baked a rhubarb pie, naturally using her own rhubarb from the previous season. Léonie has really set the bar high with this fantastic meal and tomorrow it's my turn to live up to expectations on the mountain.

Full like never before, we lean back and make plans for tomorrow. I confess to feeling a certain

trepidation about ski touring with an ex-champion, born and bred at almost 2000 metres (6562 feet) above sea level. It feels as though things could get a little sweaty.

THE NEXT MORNING we are surprised by a fantastically generous and delightful breakfast – certainly not a given in France. Apart from the obligatory baguette, there are a number of home-made jams, home-made muesli, local cheeses, local yoghurt and much more. Properly filled with energy after breakfast, we throw the skis and ski boots into the car and follow Léonie. After only a few kilometres up the valley, the road turns into a ski track. At this time of year, you cannot take a car over the Cayolle Pass and the Route des Grandes Alpes is only accessible by skis or snowshoes.

Since we have made the mistake of leaving our equipment in the car overnight, we have to wrestle a bit with stiff ski boots but, after a little pain and swearing, our feet are in and we can get going. The trek leads steadily upwards, through a pine-scented conifer forest, parallel to a babbling brook. The crowns of the trees filter the sun's rays so they reflect in the glistening snow and complete the feeling of bliss. Léonie is obviously completely unaffected by both the elevation and the sun's heat and chats as if it's already after-ski. She continues to talk about her farm, about what it was like to take it over from her parents, about what she is going grow in the coming summer season, and about her ambition to run her guest house with as many locally produced products as possible.

"We live here. There are mountains here. So we ski."

The vegetables and meat are theirs and they are good at utilising everything the farm and the forest has to offer. She would like to grow the farm, but it's hard to get workers up here. It is, quite simply, too isolated for most. Many people have a romantic image of living like this but, when the chips are down, it's a tough life that few people can manage or want to lead.

AFTER AN HOUR OR SO the forest starts to thin out and we enter an enormous open cauldron that seems to be made for skiing. Whichever way we look we see lines. Now we understand that it's here in Mercantour that the mountain guides from the big, well-known ski resorts higher up in the Alps come to when they want to be by themselves and just ski. There are no ski lifts, and the feeling of wilderness is magnificent – here you are alone on the mountain. There is something compelling and delightful about the simplicity: We live here. There are mountains here. So we ski. I understand the feeling.

After yet another hour, duty calls and Leonie must turn around. We say our farewells and see her disappear in perfectly balanced turns down the valley in that energy-saving way that only people who have grown up in the mountains use. We continue for a while longer, until a blister starts nagging. We find a fine place in the sun with a fantastic panorama over the mountains and with curiosity we unpack the food parcel that Gudrun gave us this morning. We find carefully packed, gigantic baguettes filled with the goat's cheese we dreamt of last night and sun-dried tomatoes in oil from last season. We also see that there's something that looks like a small dessert. We hope it's some of the delicious rhubarb pie that we were too full to fully appreciate last night. It turns out to be a blueberry pie which, at this moment, I guarantee is the tastiest blueberry pie I have ever eaten.

Sated and content, we prepare for the run to which we have devoted so many hours of uphill trekking to get to enjoy. A wonderful wavy run in the spring snow that we finish half an hour later, sweaty and happy, down where we parked the car, a run that was so worth all the effort.

SOON WE ARE SITTING in the car and have three hours of downhill driving back to the Mediterranean and Nice. But we already wish we were back with Léonie and Jean. Back to their hospitality, food, skiing and their contagious love of the mountains.

Merci Léonie et Jean. À bientôt Gite Ferran. ❄

RAGOUT BOLOGNESE

Long, slow cooking beats most things. Here with the undisputed king of stewing meat: chuck steak.

600 g (1 lb 5 oz) chuck steak

2 tbs olive oil

1 tsp salt

2 onions

3 garlic cloves

1 red chilli

400 g (14 oz) crushed
tomatoes

2 tbs tomato purée

300 ml (10 fl oz) water

100 ml (3½ fl oz) red wine

2 bay leaves

1 tsp dried oregano

1 tsp dried thyme

400 g (14 oz) pasta,
preferably mafaldine or
pappardelle

a good handful flat-leaf
(Italian) parsley

salt, black pepper

1. Cut the chuck in pieces, approx. 2 × 2 cm (¾ × ¾ in). Salt and brown them in the oil over a high heat until they have a golden-crusted surface.

2. Peel and finely chop the onions, garlic and chilli and fry along with the chuck for another minute or so.

3. Pour in the crushed tomatoes, tomato purée, water, wine and herbs. Simmer, covered, for approx. 3 hours or until the meat starts to fall apart. Stir now and then so that nothing burns.

4. Add salt and black pepper to taste.

5. Boil the pasta according to the instructions on the packet.

6. Stir the ragout and pasta together. Serve on the plates or on a serving platter.

Top with the shredded parsley.

ROAST SHOULDER OF PORK WITH SAUTÉED BRUSSELS SPROUTS AND MUSHROOM SAUCE

In Sweden, Sunday roast is a classic. When the roasted meat is placed on the table together with its delightful accompaniments, success is guaranteed. I often use pork shoulder since it contains quite a lot of fat, which makes the meat juicy and acts as a natural flavour enhancer.

To go with this slap-up meal, I think a slightly sweeter pale ale is a brilliant choice.

OVEN: 140°C (285°F)

PORK SHOULDER

1 tsp salt
800 g (1 lb 12 oz) piece boneless pork shoulder
½ tsp black pepper, ground
½ tsp green pepper, ground
½ tsp rosé pepper, ground
50 g (1¾ oz) butter
2 tbs cooking oil

BRUSSELS SPROUTS

300 g (10½ oz) brussels sprouts
100 g (3½ oz) butter
1 bunch chives
a handful parsley
a handful tarragon
salt

MUSHROOM SAUCE

1 onion
1 garlic clove
150 g (5½ oz) button mushrooms
150 g (5½ oz) oyster mushrooms
50 g (1¾ oz) butter
100 ml (3½ fl oz) white wine
100 ml (3½ fl oz) thick (double/heavy) cream
300 ml (10 fl oz) milk
½ tsp salt
1 tsp Chinese soy sauce
black pepper

PORK SHOULDER

1. Salt the meat on all sides. Mix the different types of pepper and roll the meat in the pepper mixture.

2. Brown the meat in butter and oil over a high heat. Put it into the oven and roast to an inner temperature of 68°C (154°F).

3. Remove the roast and let it rest while you prepare the rest of the meal.

BRUSSELS SPROUTS

1. Trim the brussels sprouts. Cut them in half and sauté in butter over a medium heat.

2. Cut the chives finely and add to the brussels sprouts. Salt to taste.

3. Top with the tarragon and parsley.

MUSHROOM SAUCE

1. Peel and finely chop the onion and garlic.

2. Clean and slice the mushrooms.

3. Melt the butter in a saucepan and fry the onion and garlic over a medium heat until soft.

4. Add the mushrooms and fry for a further 3–5 minutes.

5. Add the wine and reduce.

6. Add the cream and milk and simmer over a low heat for 10 minutes.

7. Blend the sauce with a stick blender and add soy, salt and black pepper to taste. Add more milk if the sauce feels too thick.

Carve the meat and serve with the Brussels sprouts, mushroom sauce and roast potatoes.

FRIED FLATBREAD WITH PORK AND GIROLLES

People who ask me what I like to eat may be a little disappointed when I say that I think fast food is fantastic. Just because I've worked in Michelin-starred restaurants, competed at the highest level and eaten in many of the finest restaurants, it does not mean that it's the kind of food I cook and eat at home. Quite the opposite. At home, simple food rules – sometimes fast food.

So what constitutes fast food?

For me it's a collective name for a variety of fast and simple dishes, such as hamburgers, pizza and kebabs. Here I've chosen to make a Swedish variation of a kebab with salt pork, mushrooms and lingonberries in a freshly fried flatbread.

200 ml (7 fl oz) white wine
300 ml (10 fl oz) water
2 garlic cloves
1 bay leaf
a handful thyme
1 salt-cured pork shank
salt

FRIED FLATBREAD
150 ml (5 fl oz) plain yoghurt
2 tbs golden syrup
½ tsp salt
½ tsp bicarbonate of soda
60 g (2 oz) sifted rye flour
90 g (3 oz) plain (all-purpose) flour
1 shallot
110 g (4 oz) girolles mushrooms
2 tbs butter for frying
2 tbs lingonberries or cranberries
a handful parsley

1. Bring the white wine and water to the boil with the garlic, bay leaf and sprigs of thyme.

2. Put the pork shank into the liquid, then cover and simmer for approx. 2 hours until the meat starts to come off the bone.

3. Remove the pork and pull the meat apart. Add salt to taste.

4. Combine the yoghurt, golden syrup, salt, bicarbonate of soda, rye flour and plain flour into a dough. Divide the dough into 4 pieces, roll them out and prick with a fork. Fry the bread in a dry frying pan over a high heat, approx. 1 minute per side.

5. Peel and finely chop the shallot.

6. Clean, then fry the girolles in butter until they have a good colour, approx. 5 minutes. Add salt to taste. Stir in the shallot.

7. Place the fried bread on a plate, heap on plenty of shredded pork and top with the mushrooms. Finally, add the lingonberries and sprigs of parsley.

Note!

If you can't find fresh lingonberries, frozen ones work just as well.

SWEET

LEMON MERINGUE PIE

The people's favourite and one of the most well-known desserts: lemon meringue pie. This beguiling and creamy pie takes you to the place you most want to be: heaven.

OVEN: PASTRY CASE: 175°C (345°F), FILLING: 120°C (250°F)

―――

PASTRY CASE

500 g (1 lb 2 oz) plain (all-purpose) flour

175 g (6 oz) icing (confectioners') sugar

250 g (9 oz) butter

1 egg

1 egg white

FILLING

3 lemons, juice

300 ml (10 fl oz) thick (double/heavy) cream

175 g (6 oz) sugar

4 eggs

1 egg yolk

ITALIAN MERINGUE

265g (9½ oz) sugar

4 tbs water

2 egg whites

1. Mix all the ingredients for the pastry case, using your hands, and let the dough rest in the fridge for 30 minutes.

2. Roll out the dough thinly on a floured worktop and line a pie dish with removable rim, 23 cm (9 in) in diameter. Trim the rim with a knife and prick the base with a fork for a more even surface.

3. Bake in the oven for approx. 10 minutes. Remove the pastry case and let it cool.

4. Put all the ingredients for the filling in a heatproof bowl and whisk carefully. Place the bowl over a saucepan of boiling water and warm to 60°C (140°F) while whisking continuously.

5. Strain the mixture through a fine-meshed sieve. Fill the pastry case with the mixture and bake for approx. 15–20 minutes. Let the pie cool in the fridge.

6. Boil water and sugar for the meringue over a medium heat to 121°C (250°F). Whisk the egg whites until fluffy, using an electric mixer, while the sugar syrup boils.

7. Pour the sugar syrup into the egg white foam in a thin trickle, while whisking constantly. Lower the speed of the mixer and continue whisking until the meringue has cooled.

8. Spread or pipe the meringue over the lemon pie and scorch quickly with a blowtorch, or place under the grill (broiler) on high heat for a short while.

SABLÉ BRETON WITH CARAMELISED PEACHES AND VANILLA ICE CREAM

Fruit, cake and ice cream, an unbeatable all-in-one combination that has the thing we chefs desire: different textures and temperatures. The sweet fruit swimming in warm caramel sauce, together with the slightly drier cake and a creamy ice cream add up to something very special. In this dish you get sensations of cold, warmth and crispiness.

OVEN: 140°C (285°F)

SABLÉ BRETON

2 egg yolks

90 g (3 oz) sugar

180 g (6½ oz) plain (all-purpose) flour

1 tsp baking powder

1 tsp vanilla sugar

100 g (3½ oz) butter at room temperature

½ tsp salt

CARAMELISED PEACHES

4 peaches

265 g (9½ oz) sugar

1 tbs dark rum

75 g (2¾ oz) butter

SABLÉ BRETON

1. Whisk the egg yolks and sugar together until fluffy.

2. Sift the flour, baking powder and vanilla sugar into the egg mixture and work it into a dry dough.

3. Knead the butter and salt into the dough.

4. Shape the dough into a thick roll, cover in cling film and let it rest in the fridge for 30 minutes.

5. Cut the roll into 12 slices and place on a baking sheet covered with baking paper.

6. Bake the cakes for 25–30 minutes, until golden.

CARAMELISED PEACHES

1. Halve the peaches, remove the stones and dice into pieces approx. 2 × 2 cm (¾ × ¾ in).

2. Melt the sugar in a frying pan to make a dark caramel.

3. Add the peach pieces and stir carefully.

4. Pour on the rum and add the butter. Stir and let simmer for 2–3 minutes over a medium heat so that the sugar and butter combine.

Serve the peaches straight from the pan, together with the cakes and a generous dollop of ice cream.

CHOCOLATE SEMIFREDDO WITH CARAMELISED MILK AND HAZELNUTS

Semifreddo means half frozen in Italian and it's the perfect ice cream dessert for those of you who want some luxury but don't have an ice cream machine. Here are two of my favourites: one with dark chocolate, caramelised milk, roasted hazelnuts and cocoa nibs; the other is a more refreshing kind, with lemon and cookie crumbs.

180 g (6½ oz) dark chocolate (70%), broken into pieces

3 eggs

45 g (1½ oz) sugar

300 ml (10 fl oz) thick (double/heavy) cream

125 g (4½ oz) dulce de leche

55 g (2 oz) roasted, peeled hazelnuts

2 tbs cocoa nibs

1. Melt the chocolate in a heatproof bowl over boiling water.

2. Separate the eggs, putting the yolks and whites into 2 bowls.

3. Whisk the egg yolks and sugar until fluffy.

4. Whisk the egg whites to a firm foam.

5. Whip the cream in a separate bowl.

6. Fold the melted chocolate into the egg yolk mixture. Fold in the cream, and finally the egg whites.

7. Pour the mixture into a 1 litre (34 fl oz/4 cups) container and put into the freezer for at least 5 hours.

8. Take the semifreddo out from the freezer 10 minutes before serving and cut into portions.

9. Trickle dulce de leche over each piece and top with roasted hazelnuts and cocoa nibs.

LEMON SEMIFREDDO WITH COOKIE CRUMBLE

OVEN: 175°C (345°F)

3 eggs
90 g (3 oz) sugar
400 ml (13½ fl oz) thick (double/heavy)
  cream
2 lemons, juice and finely grated zest
25 g (1 oz) butter
30 g (1 oz) plain (all-purpose) flour
3 tbs sugar

1. Separate the egg whites and yolks in
2 bowls.

2. Whisk the egg yolks and sugar until fluffy.

3. Whisk the egg whites into a firm foam.

4. Whip the cream in a separate bowl.

5. Fold the cream into the yolk mixture, then
the egg white, lemon juice and half of the zest.

6. Pour the mixture into a 1 litre (34 fl oz/
4 cups) container. Put into the freezer for at
least 5 hours.

7. Mix the butter, flour and remaining sugar
well to make a cookie crumble dough. Spread
out the dough on a baking sheet covered with
baking paper. Bake in the oven for approx.
15 minutes until golden. Let cool.

8. Take the semifreddo out of the freezer
10 minutes before serving. Top with the cookie
crumble and the rest of the grated lemon zest.

DARK CHOCOLATE CREAM WITH RUM-MARINATED BERRIES

Like a chocolate praline but served in a glass! This delightfully smooth chocolate cream is the perfect ending to an evening. Frozen berries are perfectly all right – while you're at it, make a larger amount because they only get better with time.

CHOCOLATE CREAM
200 ml (7 fl oz) milk

200 ml (7 fl oz) cream

5 egg yolks

2 tbs sugar

180 g (6½ oz) dark chocolate, chopped

MARINATED BERRIES
1 vanilla pod

175 g (6 oz) sugar

200 g (7 oz) mixed berries

200 ml (7 fl oz) dark rum

CHOCOLATE CREAM

1. Bring the milk and cream to the boil then remove from the heat.

2. Whisk the egg yolks and sugar until fluffy then fold into the milk mixture.

3. Simmer the mixture over a medium heat, whisking constantly, until it reaches 83–84°C (181–183°F).

4. Pour the mixture over the chocolate and stir until the chocolate melts.

5. Pour into glasses or bowls and place in the fridge for 24 hours.

MARINATED BERRIES

1. Cut the vanilla pod lengthways and scrape out the seeds. Mix the seeds with the sugar.

2. Alternate the berries and sugar in a glass jar. Fill up with rum so it covers the berries.

Store in the fridge for at least 24 hours.

Serve the chocolate cream with the berries and a dollop of freshly whipped cream.

SWEDISH WAFFLES

Waffles are the most common dessert in Sweden during the winter months. Anyone who tastes these will understand why. With cloudberry jam and lightly whipped cream, they not only wake up your palate but also bring back childhood memories.

75 g (2¾ oz) butter
200 ml (7 fl oz) cold, carbonated water
240 g (8½ oz) plain (all-purpose) flour
300 ml (10 fl oz) thick (double/heavy) cream
butter for cooking

1. Melt the butter and let it cool.

2. Whisk the water and flour together. Stir in the butter.

3. Whip the cream and carefully fold it into the batter.

4. Heat up the waffle iron and cook the waffles, brushing the iron with a little butter between each batch.

5. Serve the waffles with jam and lightly whipped cream.

TIRAMISU

This Italian classic dessert is not only delightfully creamy, the coffee-soaked biscuit flavoured with almond liqueur gives the tiramisu an incredible richness and character. A perfect dessert for those who do not desire too sweet a finale to their dinner.

100 ml (3½ fl oz) strong, cold coffee

2 tbs almond liqueur

12 savoiardi (sponge finger) biscuits

2 egg whites

1 egg yolk

45 g (1½ oz) sugar

250 g (9 oz) cream cheese at room temperature

150 ml (5 fl oz) thick (double/heavy) cream

1 tbs cocoa powder

1. Mix the coffee and liqueur together.

2. Place half of the biscuits in a dish, approx. 10 × 15 cm (4 × 6 in), and drip half of the coffee mixture over the biscuits.

3. Whisk the egg whites into a firm foam, then whisk in the egg yolk and sugar until everything is fluffy.

4. Fold the cream cheese into the egg mixture and stir to make a smooth mixture.

5. Whip the cream and fold it into the batter.

6. Spread half of the cream cheese mixture in an even layer on the soaked biscuits.

7. Add a new layer of biscuits and drizzle the rest of the coffee mixture over them. Finally, spread on the rest of the cream cheese mixture.

8. Sprinkle with cocoa powder and leave the dish in the fridge for at least 1 hour.

Buon appetito!

CARROT CUPCAKES

Throughout my childhood, there was always carrot cake in the family cafe. The idea of cupcakes popped up in my mind when I thought of all the buns I had been offered in the ski lift over the years and how convenient the packaging of a cupcake is when you want to pack something tasty in your rucksack.

OVEN: 170°C (340°F)
APPROX. 20 CUPCAKES
———

200 g (7 oz) butter
3 eggs
220 g (8 oz) brown sugar
1 tsp vanilla sugar
180 g (6½ oz) plain
   (all-purpose) flour
1½ tsp baking powder
1 tsp ground cinnamon
1 tsp ground cardamom
2 pinches dried ginger
3 pinches salt
310 g (11 oz) carrots, finely
   grated

FROSTING
50 g (1¾ oz) butter at room
   temperature
100 g (3½ oz) cream cheese
   at room temperature
50 g (1¾ oz) icing
   (confectioners') sugar
1 tsp vanilla sugar
grated zest of 1 lime

1. Melt the butter in a saucepan and let it cool.

2. Whisk the eggs, brown sugar and vanilla sugar in a bowl until white and fluffy. Stir in the dry ingredients.

3. Add the melted butter and grated carrots.

4. Pour the batter into the cupcake forms and bake in the middle of the oven for 10–12 minutes. Let the cupcakes cool on an wire rack.

FROSTING

1. Beat the butter and cream cheese together until fluffy.

2. Add the icing sugar and vanilla sugar and keep beating to make a nice, firm frosting.

3. Pipe the frosting onto the cupcakes just before serving and sprinkle the lime zest on top.

FRUIT CAKE

This fruit cake is like a fairy tale. It's been ever-present from sports days at school to afternoon tea, mountain hikes and get-togethers with the ski club. It is basically an ordinary sponge cake, but with its figs, bananas and almonds it provides an extra energy kick.

OVEN: 175°C (345°F)

50 g (1¾ oz) butter
100 ml (3½ fl oz) milk
2 eggs
90 g (3 oz) sugar
180 g (6½ oz) plain
   (all-purpose) flour
1½ tsp baking powder
6 dried figs
30 g (1 oz) almonds, blanched
1 ripe banana
icing (confectioners') sugar

1. Grease and flour a cake tin approx. 1 litre/18 cm (34 fl oz /4 cups/7 in).

2. Melt the butter in a saucepan. Remove from the heat and pour in the milk.

3. Beat the eggs and sugar together until fluffy.

4. Stir the flour and baking powder into the egg mixture.

5. Add the butter and milk mixture.

6. Chop the figs, almonds and banana and stir into the batter.

7. Pour the batter into the cake tin and bake in the lower part of the oven for 35–40 minutes.

8. Let the cake cool in the tin and then turn it out.

9. Dust with a generous amount of icing sugar on serving.

BANANA CAKE

Sometimes you have to boost your energy levels to cope with a long day on skis. I mostly snack on nuts and fruit, but sometimes it feels quite luxurious to have a piece of cake in my rucksack to share with friends.

OVEN: 175°C (345°F)

100 g (3½ oz) butter at room temperature
175 g (6 oz) sugar
2 eggs
300 g (10½ oz) plain (all-purpose) flour
1 tsp baking powder
1 tsp bicarbonate of soda
1 tsp ground ginger
1 tsp ground cinnamon
3 bananas
50 ml (1¾ fl oz) cold coffee

1. Beat the butter and sugar together until fluffy. Add the eggs.

2. Stir in the flour, baking powder, bicarbonate of soda, ginger and cinnamon.

3. Mash 2 of the bananas into the batter and add the coffee.

4. Line an approx. 1 litre (34 fl oz /4 cups) loaf tin with baking paper.

5. Pour the batter into the tin. Divide the third banana lengthways and place the halves in the batter with the cut side up.

6. Bake the cake in the oven for approx. 1 hour. Remove the cake and let it cool before serving.

Note!

If you don't choose to take the cake with you as "fika" (Swedish coffee and cake break), I recommend that you serve it with a large scoop of vanilla ice cream and a little chocolate sauce. You're worth it!

CHOCOLATE BALLS

As my family ran a cafe when I was growing up, I was always close to the good stuff. It was not as if my little sister and I got everything we asked – or maybe nagged – for. But the thing we were often allowed was chocolate balls. These tasty morsels have always been one of my favourites, and they have often popped up on menus in the restaurants I have worked at abroad as "Swedish fika", even though it is said that chocolate balls originated in Denmark.

100 g (3½ oz) butter
90 g (3 oz) sugar
1 tbs vanilla sugar
3 tbs cocoa powder
120 g (4½ oz) oats
2 tbs strong coffee
desiccated coconut

1. Stir all the ingredients, except for the coconut, together in a bowl.

2. Roll into balls of the desired size.

3. Roll the balls in the coconut just before serving.

The chocolate balls may be kept in the fridge for 2 weeks.

CHOCOLATE TRUFFLES WITH BRANDY

If the chocolate balls were created in Northern Europe, the chocolate truffles originated in France, the cradle of gastronomy, where I often and gladly go. My reasons for going are usually food-related, since the grand final of Bocuse d'Or – the world championships for chefs – takes place in Lyon every other year. But, of course, skiing is another obvious reason.

300 g (10½ oz) dark chocolate
100 ml (3½ fl oz) thick (double/heavy) cream
1 tsp brandy
100 g (3½ oz) butter
cocoa powder

1. Chop the chocolate coarsely and place in a bowl.

2. Bring the cream and brandy to the boil and pour over the chocolate. Stir into a smooth mixture.

3. Stir in the butter.

4. Place the mixture in the fridge for approx. 1 hour to make it malleable.

5. Remove the bowl from the fridge and roll the truffles to the desired size.

6. Just before serving, roll the truffles in the cocoa powder.

ALMOND CAKE WITH WHIPPED CREAM AND BLUEBERRIES

A sponge cake with whipped cream and berries is something most people like. In this recipe I raise the bar further with the taste of almond and brown butter. The cake is at its best when freshly baked.

OVEN: 200°C (390°F)
APPROX. 16 MUFFINS
──────

ALMOND CAKE

100 g (3½ oz) butter

4 egg whites

100 g (3½ oz) icing (confectioners') sugar

60 g (2 oz) plain (all-purpose) flour

40 g (1½ oz) almond flour

½ tsp baking powder

1 pinch salt

TOPPING

200 ml (7 fl oz) thick (double/heavy) cream

60 g (2 oz) blueberries

2 tbs maple syrup

1. Brown the butter in a saucepan (see page 13) and let it cool.

2. Whisk the egg whites and icing sugar together until fluffy.

3. Whisk the flour, almond flour, baking powder and salt into the egg mixture.

4. Add the brown butter and stir.

5. Fill the holes of a muffin tray to two-thirds of their capacity and bake for 8–10 minutes.

6. Top with the whipped cream, blueberries and maple syrup.

Note!

You can bake this batter in an ordinary 18 cm (7 in) cake tin. Grease the tin well with butter so the cake does not stick to the tin when done. Use a skewer to see if it's ready. It should come out clean.

FRUIT SALAD GRATIN

This dessert is always a hit. Choose your favourite fruits and/or berries, then top with white chocolate and muesli. Add a scoop of vanilla ice cream to the plate and you're in heaven.

OVEN: 200°C (390°F)

400 g (14 oz) fruit and/or fresh berries
100 g (3½ oz) white chocolate
70 g (2½ oz) muesli

1. Cut the fruit into pieces and put them – with the berries, if using – into an ovenproof dish.

2. Chop the chocolate coarsely and sprinkle it evenly on top.

3. Top with the muesli and cook under the grill (broiler) until the chocolate has melted and turned golden, 5–7 minutes.

4. Serve with vanilla ice cream.

WHITE CHOCOLATE PANNA COTTA WITH CITRUS AND ROASTED CHOCOLATE

Citrus fruits are at their best during the winter months and you should use this opportunity! Here I use a mixture of fresh fruits with a white chocolate panna cotta which I top with lightly roasted white chocolate for the finishing touch.

3 gelatine leaves

150 ml (5 fl oz) thick (double/heavy) cream

150 ml (5 fl oz) milk

3 tbs sugar

280 g (10 oz) white chocolate

1 orange

1 pink grapefruit

1 pomelo

1. Soak the gelatine leaves in cold water for 15 minutes.

2. Bring the cream, milk and sugar to the boil.

3. Chop 180 g (6½ oz) chocolate finely and add to the liquid.

4. Squeeze the gelatine leaves thoroughly and let them dissolve in the liquid while stirring.

5. Pour into 4 glasses and let the panna cotta set in the fridge for about 2 hours.

6. Coarsely chop the remaining chocolate and spread it thinly on a baking sheet lined with baking paper. Roast in the middle of the oven for approx. 6 minutes, until it starts to take on colour. Let the chocolate cool and then chop it into the desired size.

7. Segment the citrus fruit (see page 98) and put equal amounts into each glass of panna cotta. Top with the roasted chocolate.

SNOW FACTS

220

The world's longest cross-country ski race is the Nordenskiöldsloppet. The track is 200 kilometres (124 miles) long. It was first held in 1884, making it one of the world's oldest races. The competition starts in Jokkmokk in Lapland, Sweden.

The world's biggest elevation with cable car difference is found in Aiguille du Midi in Chamonix. From the top at 3842 metres (12604 feet) above sea level and down to the village at 1035 metres (3395 feet) above sea level, you have an elevation difference of 2807 metres (9209 feet).

The world record in speed skiing: 254.958 km/h (158.423 mph). The record was set in Vars in France by Ivan Origone of Italy in 2016.

5421

The world's highest ski lift and ski resort is a rope tow in Chakaltaya, Bolivia. The top station is situated 5421 metres (17785 feet) above sea level. This is higher than the base camp on Mount Everest.

107

The world's highest cliff drop was made in 2008, when the Norwegian Fred Syversen – by mistake – jumped 107 metres (351 feet) from a cliff. And survived. The world's highest planned cliff jump was performed by Jamie Pierre in 2006 in Wyoming, USA. It measured 78 metres (255 feet). He also made a "mute grab" in the first 10 metres (32.8 feet).

The world's first chair lift was constructed in 1936 in Sun Valley, Idaho, USA. The second and third chair lifts were also constructed there. The inventor's name was James Curran.

The place where skiing was born has been a matter of debate, but many historians agree that skiing was born in Morgedal, Norway.

The first public ski race was held in Tromsø, Norway in 1843. The first documented ski race in Sweden was held in 1877.

253.5

The world record in ski jumping is 253.5 metres (831.69 feet) and it was set in 2017 by the Austrian Stefan Kraft in Vikersund, Norway.

The oldest person to try helicopter skiing is Gordon Precious, who was 94 years and 306 days old when he was flown to a peak in the Cariboo Mountains in Canada in 2019, to enjoy an off-piste run.

The world speed record in backwards skiing: 131.23 km/h. The record was set in 2017 by Elias Ambühl.

1924

The first Winter Olympics were held in Chamonix in 1924. The first World Championships in downhill skiing were held in Mürren, Switzerland in 1931.

The Swedish Alpine Championships were first arranged in 1937.
The first ever Alpine World Cup took place in 1967.

Monoskiing first came to light in the USA at the end of the 1950s, but was not taken up by a wider audience until the 70s when the American surfer Mike Doyle started marketing the monoskis that he had designed himself. The monoski did not come to Europe until 1978 in Chamonix. Pierre Poncet and Alain Revel became the frontmen and their photographs featured on the covers of many ski magazines at the end of the 70s and the start of the 80s. Today, interest in the monoski is dwindling, even though there has recently been a slight increase in its popularity.

In 1963, the student and skateboarder Tom Sims from New Jersey decided he wanted to skateboard even during the winter and constructed a snowboard – he called it a ski board – made of wood with an aluminium base, which he waxed with candles for a better glide. Commercially, snowboarding did not pick up speed until 1965 when the board (yet again) was invented by the engineer Sherman Poppen of Michigan, USA. He named his creation the Snurfer and more than a million of them were sold.

INDEX

THANK YOU!

Firstly, I would like to give a heartfelt thank you to Patrik and Charlotte who gave me the opportunity to create my first cookbook with a fantastic team: Patrik Engström who has taken all the food photos, Charlotte Gawell who has kept everything together and served as someone I've been able to bounce ideas off throughout the entire project; Malin Bergman who edited the Swedish text, Hans Nordmark for the translation from Swedish into English: proofreader Kathy Steer and Kai Ristilä who has designed the book.

A big thank you to my family who ignited my interest in cooking and skiing, allowing me to participate in everything and widening my view of the world from childhood to the present day.

Thank you Menigo Food Hall in Årsta; Menigo Food Service; SCAN and the gang at Sundqvist; Anna-Karin from Made in Åre; Tobbe in Åre and Iris Hantverk for help with ingredients and props; the driving spirits Sofia, Tomas, Jack, Walter and Léonie for letting us visit you.

And last, but not least: thank you Olle Broström and Pi Le for your support in the kitchen.